HONEY LAKE JUSTICE

The Never Sweats of the 1860s

Tim I. Purdy

Foreword by James E. Pardee

Lahontan Images
Susanville, California

Also by the author:

Purdy's Eagle Lake

*Sagebrush Reflections: History of Amedee &
Honey Lake*

Cover: Original Lassen County, California
         Courthouse

FIRST EDITION

Lahontan Images
P.O. Box 1093
Susanville, California 96130
916-257-6747

ISBN 0-938373-08-0

Manufactured in the United States of America

DEDICATION

To Menopause Manor and Bruce . . . Thanks

TABLE OF CONTENTS

FOREWORD

We live in age of excesses - and on occasion it is good to have these pointed out, directly or indirectly, so that we can endeavor to do better the next time around. I am sure that Mr. Purdy didn't intend to preach or point the finger. However, when you read his book and are brought to realize that people brought suit to recover $63.65 for a month's lodging, $51.50 for back wages, and finally a bar bill for 23 drinks at 25¢ a drink for a total of $5.75; we can't help but reason that inflation in today's market has gone mad.

The foregoing preliminary observation is not the main theme of Mr. Purdy's book. With a broad sweep of his brush, he chronicles the workings of the Lassen Justice Court from its inception. He reminds us that the Justice Court was the people's court; the judges were laymen, and many of the early practitioners had questionable legal backgrounds. However, by and large, justice was done.

As senior member of the Lassen County Bar and a practitioner in Lassen County for forty-four years, I have observed the court and its personnel change from a layman Justice of the Peace to a lawyer Justice Court Judge.

Mr. Purdy's endeavors cover only a limited space in time. It leaves the reader asking for more. Hopefully, there will be a sequel reaching well into the Twentieth Century.

James E. Pardee, Attorney
September 9, 1993

I. HONEY LAKE VALLEY -- 1860s

Honey Lake Valley encompasses 600 square miles located in Northeastern California (though a minor portion lies in Western Nevada) and is under the jurisdiction of the County of Lassen. The Valley has an average elevation of 4,100 feet above sea level and a diverse geographic makeup. Whether a resident or visitor, few realize the unique aspect that Honey Lake Valley is where four major land masses meet--Great Basin, Modoc Plateau, Cascade Mountains and Sierra Nevada Mountains. A quick look around the contrasts are apparent with the barren mountains on the east side versus the timber slopes of the west with alkali flats, sagebrush plains and meadows found across the Valley floor. In the center of the Valley lies Honey Lake, a large shallow playa covering 103 square miles when full, though the lake goes dry in times of drought.

The Valley received its name in 1850 when Peter Lassen and his expedition came through there searching for the fabled Gold Lake. One morning while in the Valley Lassen noted a honey dew like substance on the vegetation and hence the name. When Lassen County was created in 1864, it was named for Peter Lassen, who was murdered in a 1859 mining expedition in the Black Rock Desert, Nevada.

Travellers began to come into Valley in the early 1850s along the Nobles' Emigrant Trail 1856 became a landmark year that saw permanent settlement in the Valley, the most notable being Isaac Roop's trading post which formed the nucleus of the town of Susanville.

In 1864 the moniker of "Never Sweats" was bestowed on the residents of the Honey Lake Valley--a name that stuck to them. The term originated in an article that appeared on April 30, 1864 in the *Humboldt Register* newspaper of Unionville, Nevada in which appeared the heading of "The Never Sweats," in regards to the residents of Honey Lake Valley. The basis for the name, was derived from the fact that they believed that it was so easy to make a living in the Honey Lake Valley that its residents acquired idle habits. Yet, the residents of Honey Lake fondly adopted the name and put into use such phrases as "Honey Lake Valley - Land of the Never Sweats." Though by the 1870s visitors and new residents were perplexed by this name and some of them even attempted to decipher its meaning. In 1878 one writer using the pseudonym of Rover observed what a Never Sweat was **not**: *"Honey Lakers are here designated Never Sweats. Why not because of laziness,* *sickness or old age, nor previous condition of servitude, not for lack of possession of time or money; not from any physical imperfections, imaginary or real. It is no doubt a political or religious peculiarity."*

The comment regarding politics certainly has merit. The region has a rich political history, which began as soon as the settlers arrived, due in part was the deciding factor of who possessed jurisdiction over the Honey Lake Valley.

The Sierra Nevada Mountains which frame the the Honey Lake Valley on the southwest, created a natural barrier for those residing on its eastern slope, and when winter prevailed the mountains virtually isolated them from the State of California. It was thought that these mountain's crest marked the State's eastern boundary, though it was noted the boundary was wherever the 120th meridian might lay. While it was presumed that the region fell under the domain of the Utah Territory, its authorities were far removed at Salt Lake City, a journey of some 500 miles across treacherous deserts and mountains. It was these conditions that allowed the Honey Lakers to become an independent lot. At first, neither California nor Utah thought much of the relatively sparse settlements on the east slope of the Sierra. Yet within a short time because of the increased growth caused in part by the discovery of the Comstock and formation of Virginia City and surrounding communities the politicos took interest. Neighboring Plumas County, California attempted to exercise authority over the Honey Lake Valley, while the Honey Lakers themselves were busy forming their own home rule with other regions on the eastern slopes. Prior to Congress carving the Territory of Nevada out of western Utah Territory in 1861, the Honey Lakers had been involved with four different experimental provisional governments. However, even the creation of the Nevada Territory did not resolve the issue of who had jurisdiction over of the Honey Lake Valley, since no survey had been performed--a boundary dispute between California and Nevada ensued.

While the boundary dispute lingered, the Honey Lakers took advantage of the situation and operated both California and Nevada governments, choosing whatever seemed beneficial from either side. Plumas County established a Justice Court in Susanville to serve the needs of Honey Lake Valley in November 1860 which V.J. Borrette was elected Judge. After the formation of the Nevada Territory, it was divided into nine counties one was Lake County (name changed to Roop County on December 2, 1862) which included the domain of the Honey Lake Valley. It was Judge Gordon N. Mott's duties to appoint judicial officers for District 1. Mott appointed Susanville resident, John S. Ward as Probate Judge and to preside over the Judicial affairs of Lake County. On September 3, 1862 an election was held which included Justice of the Peace for two townships in Lake County. Z.J. Brown was elected for Lassen Township and A. Evans in Union Township.

Examination of the court records reveals that Ward was the main figure in presiding over Court matters. So for a few years the Honey Lakers had their choice of courts, though both operated under the same judicial rules. Confusing? Take in account that Ward's embossed seal includes the inscription "*Commissioner of Deeds, Roop County, N.T., Susanville, Cal.*" The only difference between these two courts was the availability of a judge to hear matters. However, in certain instances in the Plumas Court, motions for dismissal would be presented citing that California did not have jurisdiction.

The jurisdiction matters were finally resolved when a formal boundary line survey was conducted during 1863/4 between the two states. The results showed Honey Lake Valley as a part of California. On April 1, 1864, the Honey Lakers, now official Californians, were provided with their own County--Lassen--carved out of eastern Plumas. In the aftermath, what little remained of Roop County died a slow death and was finally dissolved and annexed to Washoe County, Nevada in 1883.

II. MONEY MATTERS

The first case to be filed in a regular court of law in Honey Lake Valley was that of E. V. Spencer & Co. versus J. E. Shearer & Bro. The case was filed on December 15, 1860 in which Spencer sought to collect on a $190 promissory note. On December 20th the Court allowed Spencer to attach property belonging to Shearer to secure payment which consisted of eight oxen, three piles of lumber and real estate known as the Power Ranch. The following day the parties agreed to a settlement and they split the court costs of $13.75.

Spencer's case set the stage for what would be the most filed type of action in the Courts-- that is the recovery of money through promissory notes and/or services rendered. A promissory note is a written agreement between two or more people for a loan of money, with interest--rates during this era varied between 2% to 5%. These notes were a common practice of the 1860s, due in part that there were no banks. Of note: it would not be until 1892 that the first bank in

Honey Lake Valley was established and it would be formed by the individuals who had made a practice and/or living by lending money secured by a promissory note.

The average promissory note collection case was for $137.00. Yet, it did not prevent Isaac Roop from filing suit against Thomas N. Long for fifty cents. It cost Roop $2.50 to have a summons served on Long. And, yes Roop won and collected costs.

While some defaulted on their promissory notes, there were others who had the task of collection of wages and services. One circumstance was the 1866 case of *L. F. Preble vs. A. Ramsey*. Preble sued not only for $51.50 in back wages, but an additional $140 for "*damage sustained by neglect of proper attention to the ranch*." Though it was not disclosed in the court records what type of damages or injuries Preble sustained, he was awarded the full judgment of $191.50.

The Honey Lake Valley merchants had to take many of their customers to court for collection of their store accounts. In certain instances the merchants requested warrants for arrest of some the their clientele, as they feared they would leave the county--and some did escape. These instances caused a chain reaction of sorts, as the merchants were not immune from the court system. They too received a line of credit from their wholesalers and were at their mercy. The firm of M. Heller & Bro. of San Francisco sued Susanville general merchandise dealer Goldstein & Jacobs for the remaining unpaid balance of $204.60, which was a year overdue. In May, 1865 every item in Goldstein & Jacobs store was attached to secure payment.

Of course there is always a loop hole by which someone discovers a way in which not to pay. This happened to Sarah Emerson, proprietor of the Steward House Hotel in Susanville. Emerson sued A. R. Leroy in 1867 for $63.65 for lodging. The routine disposition of court procedure was followed and Emerson was awarded a judgment. With attachment in hand Deputy Sheriff Frank Peed impounded Leroy's horse. Peed then had to release the horse back to Leroy, even though he had not paid the judgment. Leroy produced his certificate as commanding officer of the Honey Lake Rangers (a calvary company organized under the National Guard of California) and was thus exempt from the execution of the attachment under military law.

Just like the merchants, the teamsters who freighted the merchandise into the valley also found themselves in a similar situation. An incident arose between Samuel Stinson and Philip Wales, and Wales' agent, M. Beanstock. Beanstock offered Wales the job of hauling Stinson's household furnishings, which was agreed upon with a discount clause for early payment of $18 before the first of March 1863, or $20 after that date. Beanstock told Wales to keep the furnishings until payment was received. Yet, Stinson was still trying to obtain his property when he brought the action against Wales on August 24, 1863. The case was delayed as Beanstock could not be found and on September 5th, Judge Young ordered Constable Naileigh to collect Stinson's property from Wales.

The mid 1860s found Susanville and the Honey Lake Valley a crossroad for traffic leading in various directions. But in the beginning, while there was considerable traffic coming there headed to the gold fields of California, the tables were reversed with an exodus from California to the mining discoveries of Idaho and Nevada.

Susanville was a strategic location for this new migration. A few enterprising entrepreneurs established the Idaho-California Fast Freight Company, incorporated and headquartered in Susanville. The company was able to obtain the government's lucrative tri-weekly mail route contract from Chico, California to Ruby City, Idaho at $45,000 per year. On July 1, 1866 the inaugural stage left Chico for Ruby City making the 427 miles trip in three days and five hours.

Even with the Company's mail contract, their creditors grew wearisome about collections. And not only were the Company's creditors nervous about receiving payment, so was the hired help. M. G. White not only worked for the Company for two months without pay, he also supplied the stage line with two horses. When White filed suit to recover $299.25 in back wages and services, there were many others who had also filed suit--some for much larger sums were filed in the Lassen County District Court.

By 1867 the Central Pacific Railroad tracks were laid across Nevada reaching Winnemucca thereby reducing the travel distance by half for the mail contract, and so the government declined to renew the contract for the Stage Company. Without the contract the Company went bankrupt, resulting in a mad scrabble to attach the few assets of the stage line.

There was the case of *J. E. Coleman vs. S. D. Howard*, in which Coleman worked for Howard for four months as teamster at $50 per month. Coleman had only received a cash credit of $11.50. In 1866, Coleman, took the matter to court for collection. After a judgment had been rendered neither party was residing in the Honey Lake Valley. Coleman moved to Indiana, and in 1868 Howard was found in Sonoma County, California, in which it was now possible to attach and collect Howard's property to pay Coleman. What transpired was that Coleman soon discovered how frustrating the collection process could be, especially via the mails. The case left a legacy of a paper trail which provides insight into this dilemma. The following letters are an illustration of what transpired.

Sheriffs Office Sonoma County
Santa Rosa
Feby 18, 1868

County Clerk, Lassen County

I send herewith execution in the case of

Coleman vs. Howard satisfied, and I have forwarded to you by Wells Fargo & Co. express the amount collected on said execution in currency, Two Hundred and Nineteen Dollars. Please send me a discharge. I do not know where the Plaintiff in the case now is, and have no authority from him to pay the money to any attorney. It was with much difficulty that I obtained the money and it was only through the assistance of an attorney that I succeeded, and I think that plaintiff ought to pay his fee $25-- Of course I have no right to retain it and must rely on the justice of the plaintiff. Please request him to send the amount to me, or if you have authority to do so remit out of the amount send you.

Respectfully,
J.O. Clark, Sheriff
Sonoma County

July 5, 1868
Washington, Ind.

Mr. A.A. Smith

Sir, I received yours of June 2nd. I was surprised to hear that I had to go through so much form of law, before I could get the money. I authorized the Sheriff of Sonoma County to collect the money and send it to E.E. Meek of Marysville, it appears to me that has put me to a great deal more trouble than any need of,

You may send Clark, the Sheriff of Sonoma County that lawyer fee of ($25) twenty five dollars currency. I dont think that he had any right to employ a lawyer at my expense to collect a judgment,

I dont understand why you charge $7.00 currency for $4.00 coin,

Inclosed I send you a power of attorney to attend to that business for me, you can put your name to it or have some responsible person to do it, the space is left blank for the name.

Pay charges out of the money and send the balance to me in Post Office money orders to Washington, Daviess County, Indiana,

I expect to return to Susanville next fall, I dont like this country.

Yours,

John E. Coleman

Sept. 13, 1868
Washington, Ind.

Mr. A.A. Smith

Dear Sir, I wrote you over two months ago, and sent a power of atty to you to put some responsible persons name to it act for me, and send me that money. I would like to know why it has not been sent. It has had ample time to come.

When you send it, if you can't send it all in my name, send some in Thos. I. Colemans name, and I will be much obliged.

Yours respectfully,
John E. Coleman

In all, total judgments were rendered for $24,458.00 Collecting the money awarded was another story, as only $1,894.69 was paid in cash. To secure payments, property--both real and personal--was attached by a lien and this kept the Sheriff and his deputies busy securing and collecting the property. Once the property was seized by an attachment, the debtor had a choice of negotiating payments or the Sheriff would sell the property at a public auction. The following is a compilation of all the property attached by the Sheriff: 87 horses and mules, 79 cows, 96 oxen, one lot of sheep, 24 wagons, 24 saddles & harnesses, one Concord Buggy, 67 tons of hay, 28,010 pounds of grain, 7,852 pounds of barley, 724 pounds of oats, 220 pounds of butter, 2,000 pounds of cheese, 55 cords of firewood, 800 board feet of lumber, one lot of saw logs, one violin, one gun, one axe, 28 sides of sole leather, one billiard table, nine ranches, eighteen town lots in Susanville, the Johnstonville Flour Mill, Thompson's rock quarry, Roop's municipal water system, the Susanville Brewery, and the Miller and Magnolia Saloons.

A final note. The Honey Lakers, survived the hard times and lack of cash, developed their own currency. In 1857 it was discovered that rutabaga turnips thrived in the Valley, and they became a form of Honey Lake currency. When Honey Lake Valley's first newspaper, the *Richmond Times*, made its appearance in April 1860, they offered a subscription price of "*200 pounds of rutabagas.*" And in at least one case rutabagas were accepted as legal tender. In 1866 when A. Dillon sued Antone Storff over the payment for labor and sundry supplies, Dillon accepted Storff's partial payment in rutabagas.

III. OUT OF BOUNDS

While there was the lingering question of who had jurisdiction over the Honey Lake Valley, it did not prevent the Never Sweats from filing law suits that were far away from the confines of the Valley, or of any Township they observed. These cases involved locales of over 100 miles to the north, east and south of Susanville, comprising a rather large territory.

The first two cases should have been handled by the authorities of Carson County, Utah Territory--the Territory of Nevada was not created until March 2, 1861.

One of the earliest recorded cases in the Honey Lake Valley is one that revolved around an accident on the toll road between Silver City, Nevada and Virginia City, Nevada. On January 1, 1861, M. W. Haviland filed suit against J. E. Shearer & Company in Judge Borrette's Plumas County Court. In November 1860 Haviland rented the Shearer Company a wagon and six oxen to haul merchandise to Virginia City. On the toll road between Virginia City and Silver

White one ton of hay at $25. White had hired
five men and two wagons to cut and remove the
hay which was worth four cents a pound. Of the
five men who actually cut and hauled of the hay,
no one could agree as to how much was cut,
citing estimates between 400 to 1,000 pounds.
After hearing the testimony Borrette rendered a
verdict in favor of Thomas Bare, not for the $199
he sought, but for only $55.

A hundred miles to north of Susanville lies
Surprise Valley--another bastion of independence
and of questionable jurisdiction. (Surprise Valley
lies in California's extreme northeast corner.
Before the creation of Modoc County in 1874,
the area was under the jurisdiction of Siskiyou
County.)

In the spring of 1864, A. R. Leroy sold an
undivided half-interest in a 160-acre-homestead in
Surprise Valley to Richard Harold. It was agreed
that Harold would cultivate and make
improvements to the property and Leroy provided
him $299 to do the work. That fall Leroy sued
Harold, claiming that he had fraudulently sold the
property to buyers unknown to him and to
recover the $299 as Harold did not fulfill the
agreement. Judge Young awarded Leroy the
judgment, but collection was a problem. W. H.
Crane, acting as Constable served the Attachment
on Harold and wrote on the proof of service
*"Served the within by levying upon two mules, one
set of harness and one wagon on 17th day of Sept.
1864, which I was prevented from removing by
threats and menacing which Deft. afterwards took*

away."

It appears that A. R. Leroy finally recovered his Surprise Valley holdings or at least acquired another one. In the fall of 1865 Leroy had sued Samuel Swearinger for ranch fees and the keeping of a horse at Surprise Valley. A judgment was awarded to Leroy for $30 and he received via the Sheriff one bay mare belonging to Swearinger for payment.

IV. LAND AND WATER DISPUTES

While money was the focus of attention in the Courts, land and water disputes also played a role in the Courts time.

There were the typical landlord-tenant disputes. A good example of this type of action can be found in the 1864 case of A. W. Hardin vs. George Wedekind. Hardin rented a house and adjoining lot to Wedekind for $5 a month. After five months had passed, Wedekind had only paid $11.00 in rent, so Hardin sued to reclaim the back rent of $28, plus damages of $20. Hardin also served Wedekind with an eviction notice, but the latter would not leave. However, Wedekind's version of the agreement differed from Hardin's affidavit. Wedekind stated that it was agreed between the two that the repairs and improvements he made to house would be deducted from the rent. Wedekind stated he had put in a new outside entrance to the house and a new gate. Wedekind claimed the cost of the improvements, including that of labor and supplies, totaled $48.87. He then counter-sued

Hardin for $23.87, the difference in the balance due on the rent. The case drug on, due in part to the creation of Lassen County--all cases being heard by Judge Ward were transferred to Judge Young who was elected Judge of the newly-created Susanville Township and it created a back log of cases to be reviewed. Three months later, Wedekind finally left the premises and the Judge ruled that Hardin was only entitled to receive $14.69 in back rent.

Then there was the less serious case of pasture for a horse. When Lafayette Marks failed to pay William Weatherlow for four months of pasturing his horse, Weatherlow sued to recover the $8 due. The case was quite simple--Marks failed to pay and Weatherlow became the owner of Marks' horse.

Emily Arnold, owner of the Susanville Hotel decided to lease the business for six months-from September 4, 1860 to March 4, 1861-to A. A. Holcomb. After the lease expired, Arnold had to go to court to evict Holcomb from the hotel. Even with the eviction notice from Judge Borrette, Holcomb refused to leave the premises. Arnold went a step further by filing a Suit of Restitution and a jury trial was held.

During the trial questions arose about the title to the property. The key witness was Isaac Roop who not only had sold the property to Emily Arnold, but had drawn up the lease between Arnold and Holcomb. With the information presented the jury returned the following verdict: "*That in as much as we have no*

power to investigate the title to the property that the
defendant shall deliver up the property to the
Plaintiff as per contract."

The leasing of ranches was a common
occurence in this era and there were a lot of
problems when it came to removing the renter
from the property. A good example of this was
the case of *Dow Vincent vs. Elijah Frost.* In
September 1863 Vincent rented his Soldier
Bridge Ranch to Frost for $5 a month, with the
understanding that he could take back possession
at any time. In February 1864 Vincent wanted to
move back onto his ranch and wanted Frost off
the premises, but Frost was not willing to move.
A month later Vincent filed two actions: to not
only have Frost removed from the premises; but
he also sought an additional $56 in back rent and
damages to the property.

In the meantime Frost responded that in
their agreement the rental fee was to be waived
for any improvements he made to the property.
Frost reported that he had made substantial
improvements to the property, including the
building of a corral and house valued at $51.
Further, Frost informed the court that Vincent
owed him $10 for work he performed the
previous fall as a teamster. Frost's attorney, E.
V. Spencer, attempted to delay the proceedings.
Spencer first requested from Judge Ward that a
dismissal be granted as Justice Courts under the
California Constitution did not have the authority
to hear matters of unlawful detainers. Ward
denied Spencer's motion for dismissal. Next,

Spencer then stated that his client could not receive a fair and impartial trial before Judge Ward, though he did not cite any reason, and this too was denied.

A jury trial was held in which a split verdict was rendered. The jury awarded Frost $10 and Frost was allowed to remove his blacksmith shop and a horse from the premises. In the end it was a terrible financial loss for Frost as he had to pay the court costs in the matter, which totaled $140.75.

The fight for water in the arid west has been an issue since the land was settled for agriculutral and mining purposes. The first local case was filed in 1861 between Antone Storff and "Dutch Johnny" Tucker. Storff stated that in April 1860 he cut a ditch across government land making a diversion ditch from Lassen Creek to be used for mining, agricultural and household purposes. In September 1861 Tucker turned the water off from Storff's ditch. Tucker's attorney, John S. Ward requested the matter be dismissed as justice courts have no jurisdiction in determining water rights. Judge Borrette disagreed and stated it was a matter of real property damages. Ward objected to the Judge's decision and stated he would take that matter to the Supreme Court if necessary. Next, Storff requested a jury trial, but Ward stated that his client could not receive a fair and impartial trial with Judge Borrette presiding. Borrette overruled Ward, stating that Storff demanded a jury trial and so he would not be deciding the case.

The jury was summoned and witnesses subpoenaed. During the trial it was revealed that David Titherington had purchased the property on which Storff's ditch was located from Peter Lassen's estate. Further there was an agreement between Titherington and Storff which stated he could use the water when it was not in use-- information Storff neglected to include in his complaint. The testimony was overwhelmingly against Storff and the jury returned a verdict in favor of Tucker. Storff was now not only left high and dry without water, but he had pay $65 in court costs.

V. CRIMES COMMITTED AND SUBMITTED

Honey Lake Valley had a reputation as a place where desperadoes and others of that ilk could seek shelter from prosecution. This was partly due to the political jurisdiction question as to who could exercise authority. Yet when a crime was committed in the Valley, the Never Sweats took proper control in handling the proceedings.

Being charged and arrested for stealing a horse was not such a tragic plight, as one did not end up a victim of a hanging, contrary to popular folklore. The results of such an event could be quite surprising.

In 1863 when Benjamin B. Painter was arrested for stealing a horse from A. W. Mitchell of Butte County, California Painter was found not guilty. In turn, Judge Young fined Mitchell $11 in court costs for bringing an action without sufficient information and/or evidence. While there were a dozen or so cases on this topic, if found guilty, the person accused, made restitution

and paid a fine of $25; but in most cases they
were like Painter, where someone just did not
have all the facts.

Other animals also had a way of being
found on someone else's premises. In February
1867, Joseph Myers was arrested and tried for
stealing a Black Barron hog valued at $17. The
jury found him guilty and "*recommended mercy of
the court as he is a young man, and this being his
first offense*." However, there is no record as to a
fine being imposed on Myers. Though in the case
of C. S. Whitney who was charged in November
1863 for stealing a dog belonging to William
Wentworth, it was a simple case. Whitney was
brought before Magistrate Young, pled guilty and
fined $17.

While thefts were one matter, assaults
were another. Most of the fights seem to have
originated inside or outside the areas of many
saloons. These case were quickly taken care of in
court and if the party or parties were found guilty
a fine was imposed of $25 but on rare occasions
the Judge included jail time. Most of the minor
cases were rarely tried, the defendants pleading
guilty and paying their fines. However, William
Walker was found guilty of beating up William
Corse with a club in September 1864 and in
addition to a fine he also received 40 days in jail.
Since Lassen County was still in its infancy, it had
no jail, and Walker was taken to Plumas County
for his confinement. Then, there is this amusing
anecdote found in the case of Isaac Roop who
was charged with the assault of William Hamilton

in October 1864. Judge Young provided this specific instruction to the jury: ". . . *and the Court also instructs the Jury that drunkenness cannot excuse the defendant* [Roop] *for the commission of any crime.*"

Yet the court had to deal with one repeat offender, namely Lafayette "Lafe" Marks, a Susanville teamster. On December 9, 1863 Lafe Marks made his debut appearance in Court when he hit A. Seaman with a foreign object slung from a sling shot. Marks pled guilty as charged and fined $25 which he paid. During 1865 and 1866 he was brought before the Judge on three occasions for beating up James Mennefield, William Miller and Czar Giddings, for which he was found guilty and sentenced. Lafe Marks' next offense occurred on March 31, 1867, when he attempted to shoot Joseph Myers, a much more serious offense. In this instance Myers also shot at Marks, and he too was charged, but found not guilty. Marks was not so fortunate, for he was found guilty and received a fine of $300. Marks would land in Court two more times, both assault charges: the last time in 1875 when he used a cribbage board to hit Henry Fisher.

The case, or cases, of John Webb and his subsequent actions landed him in confinement because of a unique set of events. It started on October 24, 1862 when John Ward sued John Webb to collect on a promissory note of $25 plus interest at 2%--an additional $3.40. A judgment was rendered in favor of Ward, and Webb had to pay an additional $28.50 for court costs, for which

Constable C. E. Alvord took into possession Webb's horse "Stonewall" and a bridle for security until payment could be made. On October 27th, Webb filed suit against Constable C. E. Alvord for $70, for use and damages to his horse. At first Alvord requested a dismissal in the matter, then changed his mind, and counter-sued Webb. On November 3rd, a hearing was held and Judge Young dismissed the case and imposed court cost on Webb in the amount of $27.50. Alvord, as Constable, seized one chest of carpenter tools belonging to Webb which was to be held until payment was made. After court was dismissed, Webb beat up his attorney, E. V. Spencer for losing the two cases. The next day, Spencer had criminal charges filed against Webb, who was duly arrested and brought to trial on November 5th. After considerable deliberation the jury failed to reach a verdict. Judge Young excused the jury and called for a new trial and summoned prospective jurors for the next day. However the trial did not take place as Judge Young wrote in the court docket *"During the night of Nov. 5 the Defendant escaped from the custody of the Constable."* It is unknown however, whether Webb made his escape on his own horse.

On the other hand there were some serious offenses that resulted in attempted and/or murder charges, though the outcome of the cases were different.

The earliest case tried in a regular court of law in Honey Lake Valley was that of George Hyde. Hyde was accused of assault with a deadly weapon, with the intent to commit murder. In Susanville on December 21, 1862 George Hyde walked out of the Humboldt Exchange Saloon crossed the street, drew his pistol and shot Charles Seaman in the breast. A few days later Seaman subsequently died from the injuries he sustained. While the court records do not reveal what provoked Hyde to shoot Seaman, an account is related in *Fairfield's Pioneer History of Lassen County*, which states that Hyde's action was caused by the advances made by Seaman to Hyde's wife. Hyde so stated this in court when he pled not guilty giving the justification of self defense. Hyde then requested a dismissal of the charges citing that Justice Young's Honey Lake Township, Plumas County Court had no jurisdiction as this was not a part of California. Judge Young overruled the motion and a hearing was held on the 23rd of December. After examination of witnesses Judge Young rendered that Hyde be held to answer for the crime of assault with a deadly weapon with the intent to commit murder and bail was set at $3,000. There are no records of any further proceedings and according to Fairfield, Hyde was never brought to trial or punished in any way.

Nearly a year later in Janesville David Lowrie was found guilty in the stabbing of S. E. Phillips and he received five months in the Plumas County Jail at Quincy. In 1865 two murders occurred--one in Janesville and one in Susanville. In the first case, William Walker was shot at Blanchard's Saloon in Janesville by John

Brunty. Walker was a quarrelsome fellow, who accused Brunty of meddling in the Walker family affairs. A scuffle ensued and Brunty shot Walker who died a few hours later. After a hearing Brunty was exonerated, the court stating it was justifiable homicide.

The case of John Biddle who provoked a fight with John Williams at the Pioneer Saloon in Susanville in April, 1865, proved deadly for him. Biddle had called Williams a coward, and in turn Williams knocked Biddle to the floor and kicked him several times. Apparently Williams must have kicked Biddle in a vital spot, as he died a few days later. Williams, a young man, was so frightened and startled over the affair he left the area immediately and a warrant for his arrest was issued, but it could not be served as he had fled the area.

Domestic violence is an age-old issue. Jesse Williams went before Judge Borrette on January 19, 1861 seeking the arrest of Jerry Tyler stating that Tyler's wife, Elizabeth, was deadly ill which was caused by the abuse of her husband. Williams contended in his statement that Tyler had threatened to kill his wife and he would not allow anyone to attend to her. A warrant was issued for the arrest of Tyler and Jerry and Elizabeth Tyler both appeared in court on January 21st. Elizabeth Tyler filed an affidavit stating "*She is not afraid of her life being taken by Jerry Tyler. That she is not in a dangerous condition and that her life is not in danger.*" Jerry Tyler then asked the Judge that the charges be

Magnolia Saloon, shown on the left, served as the area's first court room, until a courthouse was built in 1867--*Lassen County Historical Society*

Ephraim V. Spencer, his career in law spanned five decades--*Ivajean Wheeler*

Steward House Hotel, Susanville, was well known for its operation of faro games--*Lassen County Historical Society*

Isaac N. Roop, founder of Susanville and attorney-at-law, among his many titles--*Lassen County Historical Society*

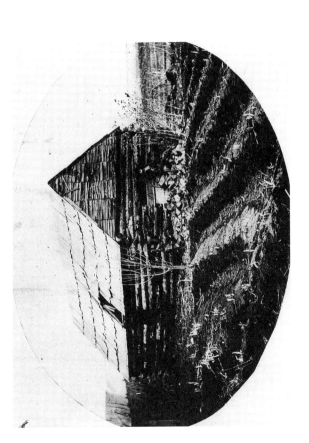

Roop's Fort, Susanville, *circa* 1870, site of the Sagebrush War--*Nevada Historical Society*

A promissory note from the case of *Hosselkus & Harvey vs. Louis Goior*

Lafayette Marks made regular appearances in the Justice
Court--*Helene Andrews*

Gay Street, mid 1860s, near the heart of Susanville--*Gil Morrill*

Richmond, _____ 186_

Mr W.T.C. Elliott

Bought of **DRAKE & PIERCE,**

DEALERS IN

GROCERIES, PROVISIONS, LIQUORS, CLOTHING, BOOTS, SHOES,

STAPLE AND FANCY DRY GOODS, &C.

After 30 days, 2 1-2 per cent. per month Interest will be charged.

1860

		Amount Brought forward	$ 138.83
Aug	23	1 pr Slippers	2.00
"	"	1 " Shoes	2.50
Sept	5	1 "Bot" Eye Water	.75
Dec	28	1 pr Blk Mitts	.75
"	29	4th Yds Wool Delane	2.66

Richmond store account of W.T.C. Elliott from *Drake & Pierce vs. W.T.C. Elliott* dropped on these grounds, which was granted. Elizabeth Tyler left her husband five months later. On June 29, 1861 she filed for divorce in the Plumas County District Court on the grounds of her husband's cruel and inhuman treatment and threats to kill her. The divorce was granted.

In the case of *People vs. Richard Thompson*, it is the final outcome of the case that is of interest. Richard and Margaret Thompson were an elderly Irish couple who resided a few miles south of Susanville. It seems Margaret was rather upset about their daughter Sarah who had recently left home to marry Thomas Mulroney. On the evening of March 12, 1867 a drunken domestic dispute occurred in which Richard Thompson attacked his 65-year-old wife Margaret with a hatchet, and the blows proved fatal.

Richard Thompson was found guilty of murder in the first-degree and was sentenced to death by hanging at San Quentin. The case was appealed to the California Supreme Court, which affirmed the Lassen County judgment and directed the Court to set a day for his execution. Since the appeal process had been exhausted, the Court set December 18, 1868 for the execution of Richard Thompson. But, in October 1868 a petition which not only sought postponement of the date of execution, but requested a commuted sentence circulated and signed by a majority of the Honey Lakers was forward to California Governor H.H. Haight. It was their intent to have the charges reduced to second-degree murder so Thompson's sentence would be life in prison. The Honey Lakers tactics proved beneficial as the Governor postponed the execution to review the material submitted by the Honey Lakers. On January 6, 1869 Governor Haight commuted Thompson's sentence to second-degree murder and sentenced him to life in prison. Though somewhat ironic, in late January 1869 when Sheriff T.N. Long transported Thompson to San Quentin to begin his sentence, Thompson remarked that he would rather be incarcerated there than turned loose here.

Thompson's case was resurrected one more time. On July 5, 1872 his son-in-law, Thomas J. Mulroney filed a notice in the Second Judicial District Court made an application Governor Booth requesting a pardon for Thompson. Mulroney stated that although the murder was done in a fit of crazy intoxication, it was unexcusable. He went on to plea that Thompson was now approaching 70 years-of-age, had not only been a model prisoner but that at this age he was harmless. It was heavily stressed that due to Thompson's age and poor health that he should spend the few remaining days in the care of his only daughter. The appeal process was lengthy, but successful--in March 1874 Governor Booth granted an executive pardon to Richard Thompson, he was released and returned to make his home in the Honey Lake Valley. However, Thompson's health greatly improved upon his return, and he lived another 21 years, dying at the age 91 in 1895!

The case of Atlas Fredonyer was one that

shocked the community due in part to his high profile. Fredonyer is credited with the 1850 discovery of a low-level pass located fifteen miles west of Susanville, which today bears his name. In 1857 he moved to what is now known as Susanville and was prominent in the affairs of the Honey Lake Valley. In that same year, the twenty-two residents who comprised the nucleus of Susanville signed a resolution declaring the place be named Fredonyer City, as no formal name had been established. (In 1858 the name of Susanville was adopted. It received its name from Susan Roop, the daughter of the town's founder, Isaac Roop.) Plumas County had offered Fredonyer the position of Justice of Peace for the Honey Lake Township, but he turned that down because for his respect of the anti-Plumas sentiment.

In spite of all of Fredonyer's involvement with the early settlement of the region, it was the charges filed against him and the subsequent actions for which he is most remembered. On December 17, 1861, Fredonyer requested a search warrant from Justice Arnold of the Brannan House Hotel in Susanville. Fredonyer suspected that his fifteen-year-old step-daughter Sally, was staying there. The search took place and Sally Fredonyer and all her belongings were found at the Brannan House.

Thus the story unfolds as to why Sally Fredonyer had sought refuge. Atlas Fredonyer was charged and went to trial accused of incestuous and criminal assault upon Sally.

Fredonyer choose to represent himself when his case was tried on May 12, 1862 at Quincy. The Plumas County District Attorney is said to have presented such a strong case that ". . . *carried conviction to the mind of every juror.*"   In his defense, Fredonyer, presented a very long verbose argument, which became known as "Fredonyer's Talk Against Time." While Fredonyer debated his defense, his erstwhile cellmate--supposedly a criminal from Honey Lake--was digging a tunnel to freedom under the County Jail.   However, the other prisoners in the jail noted the fresh earthly smell coming from Fredonyer's cell and alerted the Sheriff.   The nearly completed tunnel was discovered and the escape aborted.   Fredonyer, who was still debating case in the courtroom, ended his plea abruptly when the news of the attempted escape arrived there. Fredonyer was found guilty and sentenced on the scene receiving six years in prison.

While the evidence against Fredonyer was described as "conclusive and damning," on November 26, 1863 he received a pardon from Governor Leland Stanford. This was due in part to a petition circulated by James Duesler. The Governor noted, ". . . *circumstances have since occurred to leave a strong doubt in the minds of the Judge, District Attorney and several prominent citizens, and in consideration of his previous good moral character.*"   The editor of the *Quincy Union* was outraged by the Governor's action stating that any person who heard the trial or knew the particulars in the case could not see any injustice.

Fredonyer was released from prison, and was never to be seen in these parts again. However, Fredonyer still has the lasting legacy of three mountains and a pass that bear his name.

There were other concerns of a criminal nature that occupied the Court's time, one of which was gambling. Lassen County's first District Attorney, E. V. Spencer, took to the task of ridding Susanville of the operation of the popular but illegal faro games being conducted. (Faro is a card game in which the players bet on the order that cards will be drawn from a box.) Spencer, who was only admitted to practice law in 1862, was still learning the profession and found himself in a quandary in his attempt to rid the town of gambling, which was only a misdemeanor offense. On Valentine's Day 1865 he filed charges against George P. Heap, Joseph Hale, Charles H. Drum, J. I. Steward, William Van Kirk, Joseph Baker and John Anderson who were all conducting faro games in Susanville. At first Spencer was effective, since two of the accused left town but one did leave an imprint on Spencer for life. The first to flee was John Anderson. John Baker soon followed Anderson's departure, but not until after he had a confrontation with Spencer. There was a stand off between the two men in the dining room of the Steward House Hotel. What finally ensued was that Baker threw a large coffee cup at Spencer, which hit him on the forehead, cutting him and leaving a permanent scar. It was believed that whole incident was premeditated on Spencer's part, to provoke Baker, and Spencer was ready to shoot Baker in self-defense, though when Baker stood up at the dining table, he was unarmed. Baker left for parts unknown before he could be arrested for the assault.

As to the remaining individuals charged with gambling, their attorneys were astute to the matters at hand. These attorneys considered that the actions taken by Spencer should have never occurred--that the faro games were practically a way of life found on the frontier. Spencer presented the cases to the Lassen County Grand Jury to seek indictments, which they did. The defense counsel waited until trial to request a dismissal on the grounds that one of the Grand Jury members, namely Antone Storff, was not a United States citizen, and thus the charges were dismissed by Judge I. J. Harvey. Spencer summoned the Grand Jury at once, but the second time they failed to indict anyone.

Finally, Honey Lake Valley was not immune to the strife the nation was suffering from the Civil War.

One particular region of the Valley was more pronounced of these affairs and resulted in the giving that district the name of the Tule Confederacy. This region comprised the area southeast of Standish, though the term is used rarely today. The evolution of the name resulted when John M. Kelley settled there in 1859, coming from his native state of Missouri. In 1863, the United States Government surveyed the region, and only allowed an individual to claim 160 acres. Kelley found himself in a predicament and his holding was a great deal more than 160 acres and was worried that he would be losing a substantial part of his holdings. Kelley wrote fellow southerners, William Brashear, Robert Briggs, Chappell Kelley and John Salling to come to Honey Lake Valley and settle on the lands he had already claimed, to keep his place in tact, which they did. In 1864, Lassen County Surveyor, E. R. Nichols was doing work in the region and noted the number of southerners in the area who had also served in the Confederate Army on which he dubbed the region the Tule Confederacy. (The term tule is derived from the tule plant which flourishes in this region.)

The first incident to spark tensions over the Civil War was when Charles Mulkey was charged on November 9, 1863 for open and boisterous cheering on the streets of Susanville for Jefferson Davis, President of the Confederate States. Criminal charges were filed against Mulkey and he pled guilty before Judge Young who fined him $25.00.

Meanwhile down in the Tule Confederacy matters became a bit more turbulent. The region was experiencing quite an influx of settlers, causing boundary disputes and claim jumpers. DeWitt Chandler had his problems with these skirmishes with his neighbors George and John Purcell. The first incident occurred on December 22, 1863 when George Purcell was burning tules when the fire spread and destroyed one of

Chandler's hay stacks. It was Chandler's contention that the fire was intentional, and related to Purcell's loyalty to the Confederate States. Purcell was arrested and brought to trial where a jury found him not guilty. The following spring John Purcell set fire to Chandler's house claiming it as a victory for the Confederate States! However, there is no record of the results in the charges on the incident. Yet, there is irony in the tale and that is that in August 1864, John Purcell lodged a complaint with the District Attorney seeking the arrest of John H. Harbin who publicly denounced the United States and proclaimed allegiance to the Confederate States.

Such incidents slowly subsided after the Civil War and by the mid 1870s none of the original southern sympathizers were residing in the Tule Confederacy.

VI. TAX MAN COMETH!

To understand this chapter, one has to be aware of the political conditions found in the Honey Lake Valley. The main focus is that the settlers wanted to govern themselves, and had felt that way since they first set foot there. While boundary disputes and the Sagebrush War are a complete story in their own right, the following presentation will enlighten the reader to the facts surrounding them and that of the tax collector.

Only a month after settlement of the Honey Lake Valley had begun in earnest, the area's first form of government had been created. On April 26, 1856 a meeting of twenty men at Roop's House created the Territory of Nataqua. This territorial government was a means for the new settlers to protect their property rights and to settle land disputes through arbitration.

Nataqua Territory had a very brief life, but it was followed by other attempts to form territorial governments. It was originally presumed that Honey Lake Valley was not a part of the State of California--a logical theory was that the Sierra Nevada Mountain Range created a natural eastern boundary. When the State of California was created in 1850, the eastern boundary followed the 120th Meridian, but since it had never been surveyed no one was sure where the boundary might be.

Anyhow, at the close of the year 1856, 36,840 acres of land had been claimed in the valley with approximately 15,000 acres under cultivation in hay, grain and vegetables.

Honey Lake Valley continued to experience additional growth in 1857, so that the Plumas County Board of Supervisors exercised their authority in claiming this territory. At that Board's meeting of August 4, 1857 they created the Honey Lake Valley Township. The action did not set well with the Honey Lakers who met *en masse* to protest the Township action on August 29th. As a result of this meeting, a resolution was adopted opposing any control of Plumas County over the affairs of Honey Lake Valley.

After this event a piece of popular local folklore began, as to how the Honey Lakers evaded paying taxes to anyone. The news of the Honey Lakers' meeting had spread and the *Marysville Express* newspaper of Marysville, California noted:

"The citizens of Honey Lake Valley are, for the most part, as violently opposed as ever by the exercise of any jurisdiction over them by the authorities of Plumas County. There is, however, some with inconsistency in their conduct, for when the tax collector of Plumas County came among them, they told him they were not in California, but in Utah, and when Orson Hyde from Salt Lake visited them, they said they lived in California. . . ."

As distasteful as it might be, Plumas County assessed the lands in Honey Lake Valley to be worth $76,777 in 1858 and noted its population as 250. Growth continued in the Valley and by 1860 the census for Honey Lake Valley Township, Plumas County listed, 476 inhabitants--the figure negotiable. To determine a more accurate head count, one has to also examine those residents counted in the Long Valley Township of Carson County, Utah Territory. Whatever the numbers have been, Plumas County officials were aware that the area represented nearly 10% of the County's population and that it possessed a burgeoning tax base.

Though it appears that while Plumas County asserted authority in levying taxes, collections were another matter--which some Honey Lakers paid while others did not.

As if the Honey Lakers were not having enough problems with property taxes, they found themselves in a predicament over the business license tax. In the case of *People vs. David Blanchard*, Plumas County Sheriff-Tax Collector

E. H. Pierce filed suit on November 18, 1862 to obtain $7.50 plus an additional $15 in damages from Blanchard who failed to procure a business license for his store at Janesville. Blanchard was served with a summons to appear in court on November 26th, but he did not do so. A judgment was entered against him by default for $22.50 plus costs, and the final total came in at $39. While the Plumas authorities had a judgment against Blanchard, collection was another matter. R. York Rundell, acting as Constable noted in his attempt to attach Blanchard's property for the judgment: *"I attempted the execution of the within writ and that the execution thereof was resisted by David Blanchard to such a degree that I was obliged to desist."* End of case.

However, Tax Collector Pierce had better luck with his next case in which he filed suit against S. Friedman who failed to obtain a liquor license. While the license fee owed by Friedman was $7.50; when he appeared in Court to pay the demand, his total bill for court costs and constable fees cost him $47.50, which he paid.

While Plumas County was making futile attempts to exercise authority over the Honey Lakers, a lot was brewing on the other side of the "border." After numerous attempts to create a new government out of the western Utah Territory, Congress finally approved the formation of the Nevada Territory on March 2, 1861. On November 25, 1861 the Nevada Legislature divided its territory into nine counties, one of which was the County of Lake, which included Honey Lake Valley. Two days later the legislature appointed three Honey Lakers (William Weatherlow, William Hill Naileigh and Daniel Murray) to organize the County. These gentlemen were to arrange and supervise an election of officers for January 14, 1862, but failed to do so. Another election was scheduled and held on September 3, 1862 for Lake County officials. This was a dual election day, as Plumas County was having an election for its officials. In Janesville, diplomacy in action was found at David Blanchard's store. In opposite corners of the store, elections took place for officials for the two counties, with many a Honey Laker voting for both sets of officers!

Tension over the boundary dispute continued as to what political entity controlled Honey Lake Valley. The Nevada Territorial Legislature showed its support to retain the region on December 2, 1862 when that body changed the name of Lake County to Roop County. The climax of the situation came with the event of the one day Sagebrush War in Susanville on February 15, 1863. A half day shoot out occurred between the Plumas and Roop County forces, resulting in three injuries, one of which would be costly. A truce was declared that afternoon, a peace treaty negotiated and later appeals were sent to the Governors of California and Nevada seeking intervention and a settlement.

The settlement called for a joint survey of

the California- Nevada Territory boundary. J. F. Houghton representing California, and Butler Ives representing Nevada, were commissioned to lead the survey party, with John F. Kidder selected as Engineer-in-Chief. Their first act was to survey the 120th Meridian from Lake Tahoe to the Oregon border. The result was the Honey Lakers worst nightmare come true, as the survey officially placed them conclusively in California and under Plumas County's jurisdiction.

Undaunted by this fact, the Honey Lakers pursued one more avenue. One of their main objections to being part of Plumas County was the isolation from the County seat of Quincy (created by the mountains), as they were usually cut off entirely during the winter months, being literally snowbound.

On April 1, 1864 the California Legislature created the County of Lassen from portions of eastern Plumas and Shasta counties. (It is interesting to note that on April 4, 1864, California accepted the boundary survey results known as Kidder & Ives.) The act creating the newly-formed Lassen County required it to pay Plumas County $2,500. One thousand dollars of this sum was paid to William Bradford, whose thigh was shattered by a gunshot in the opening rounds of the Sagebrush War.

In Lassen County's first year of operation, the County had a total assessed valuation of $239,558 in land improvements and $439,301 in personal property. The County had an original tax rate of $1.25 on each $100 assessed value for

County purposes, plus collected another $1.25 on each $100 assessed value for State purposes. The total collection in taxes amounted to $16,971.47 of which the County received $8,485.57 with which to operate.   The County also had to negotiate payments to Plumas County to pay off its $2,500 debt.

When it came time to collect property taxes, Lassen County was experiencing its own problems with delinquency. Economic conditions had declined and a number of tax payers abandoned their property and moved to areas with better prospects. Then there were others, who were either accustomed to not paying or could not pay their property taxes, and/or who were taken to court.

Lassen County District Attorney, E. V. Spencer had the task of filing charges in an attempt to collect delinquent taxes.   For the County's first year in operation, Spencer attempted to collect $958.95 in back taxes, which represented nearly eleven per cent of the County's budget. These cases ranged from A.H. Hardin who owed ninety cents in the special assessment levied by the Janesville School District to $164.60, which Isaac Roop owed on his municipal Paiute Creek Water System.

In one of these tax suits a unique situation occurred when Constable E. R. Nichols sought to serve Captain William Weatherlow with a summons for $46.30 in back taxes. Nichols noted on the summons of his attempted service of February 7, 1865 that he was unable to serve

Weatherlow as he ". . . *cannot be found in the County.*" If only Nichols, who doubled as County Surveyor, had toured the Susanville Cemetery, he would have located Weatherlow's grave, as Weatherlow had died on July 22, 1864 and thereby became a permanent resident of Lassen County. It wasn't as though Nichols was unaware of who Weatherlow was--he being prominent in the affairs of the Valley--but Nichols had sued him in 1861 over a mining claim in the Black Rock Desert.

VII. TRIVIAL MATTERS

Compiling a work of an historical nature, there are those bits and pieces of information that for one reason or another do not lend themselves to the rest of the text. Instead of excluding them entirely, we devote this small section to some of the unusual court cases; and to a couple of non-related matters found in the court records.

We begin with Susanville's founder Isaac Roop, who seemed to have had certain problems with animals. On August 21, 1863, he filed suit against C. E. Alvord, who he said "*has perpetuated a nuisance by leaving in the town of Susanville the carcass of a mule*" and sought $100 in damages. Alvord appeared in Court later that day and since he had the dead mule removed the case was withdrawn, but he still had to pay $6 in court costs.

Five days later, Roop filed suit against one Seaman, first name unknown, again seeking $100 in damages as Seaman had allowed his hogs to run at large in the town of Susanville. The suit was withdrawn the next day as Seaman could not be found to be served. However, this turned out to be a re-occurring problem for Roop, as he also sued Hiram Teft in 1864 for allowing his hog to run at large in the town of Susanville. In this instant, Roop cites his concern as the owner of the town's water system which consisted of open ditches diverted from nearby Paiute Creek. In his complaint Roop stated that on May 24, 1864 and other diverse times that Teft's hog "*has entered and wallowed in pltfs. [plaintiff's] said water ditch and has urinated and deposited his excrements therein whereby the water running in the said ditch has been muddied and rendered filthy and make unfit for use . . .,*" although this time Roop only sought $50 in damages and loss of water sales. However, there is no documentation as to the outcome of this case.

It should be noted that Roop died in 1869 but his hog problem would soon be resolved. In 1870 the California State Legislature passed the Barnes Hog Law, specifically for the town of Susanville which prohibited hogs running at large!

On the topic of animals there is the case of *Valentine J. Borrette vs. W.C. Kingsbury, William Corse and W.K. Beek.* In this 1864 action Borrette claimed that Kingsbury had unlawful possession of a three-year-old cow and demanded that the cow be returned to him and claimed damages of ten dollars. What is somewhat amusing in this case is the testimony of Mary Cheney who gave a complete history of the cow, the cow's mother and who milked them. While

Borrette won his case, the defendants' appealed the judgement to the County Court and there it was dismissed in the fall of 1864 for lack of action by any of the parties.

And the final topic of the animal kingdom is that of horse racing, a popular past time of the era. A classic example was the 1864 case of *A. H. Nelson vs. James Deeds*. On January 10th, a horse race was held in which a bet of $13.50 was made between Nelson and Deeds. Nelson's horse won and not only did Deeds refuse to pay, but he had also run up a bar bill at Nelson's establishment-- twenty three drinks at twenty five cents a drink for a total of $5.75!

The establishment of toll roads in the frontier West was difficult and not usually a feasible business venture--unless you were strategically located at a bridge, mountain pass or narrow canyon where possible toll users could make a detour and thus not pay the toll fee. On several occasions toll road companies were formed for various routes leading through the Honey Lake Valley, but were never successful enterprises.

Another California neighbor of the Honey Lakers was that of Tehama County. In 1863 he Board of Supervisors of that County decided to construct, operate and maintain a toll road from its county seat of Red Bluff to Susanville. A convenient location for the toll gate was placed at Devil's Corral along the Susan River, five miles west of Susanville. In August 1864 Aaron Seaman and Jerry Tyler acting as agents for

Tehama County as toll collectors, sued John Packard and Archibald Boyd for a total $41.25 in toll charges. The toll fees were 3 cents a head for cattle, 25 cents per horseman and 50 cents per wagon. However, the resourceful Honey Lake defendants were able to have the cases dismissed. The dates of their toll fees for use of the road in August, 1864 stating that Tehama County could not collect toll fees outside their jurisdiction, since Devil's Corral was part of the newly formed Lassen County.

Found in between court proceedings of the Honey Lake Township, Plumas County Court Docket was the recording of two marriages occurring in the Honey Lake Valley. It should be noted that the first marriage in Honey Lake Valley took place on September 23, 1857 when Isaac Coulthurst and Mary Jane Duvall were united in matrimony. Marriages in the early years of settlement were rare, since the valley consisted of a large male population and eligible females were scarce. However, a most peculiar thing happened over the mountains in the Quincy, Plumas County seat. While a few of the early Honey Lake marriages are recorded there, for some odd reason from mid-1859 to 1866, there are no marriage recordings county wide. The recordings in the court docket are the only record of these marriages and are transcribed here for the record:

MARRIAGE CERTIFICATE
This is to certify that Franklin S. Strong

and Louise Jones were with their mutual consent lawfully joined together in holy matrimony, which was solemnized by me in presence of credible witnesses.

s/ Franklin S. Strong
s/ Louise C. Strong

Witnesses   )
L.H. Breed   )
E.G. Bangham)

Given at Honey Lake Valley this 15th day of Sept. A.D. 1861

V.J. Borrette
Justice of Peace

MARRIAGE CERTIFICATE

This is to certify that Jacob Hardesty and Mary Petty were with their mutual consent lawfully joined together in holy matrimony which was solemnized by me in presence of credible witnesses.

s/ Jacob Hardesty
s/ Mary Petty

Witnesses)
William Rooks)
Milly Rooks)
Charles Faulkner)

Given at Honey Lake Valley this 19th day

of Jan. A.D. 1862

C. Arnold
Justice of Peace

One of more unusual cases to surface was that of local stonemason, H.F. Thompson. At the west end of Susanville a deposit of rhyolite tuff rock was discovered in 1860. This rock became the basic building material and was used for a variety of construction purposes. It was the only stone available at that time to make cemetery markers. This brings us to the case of *H. F. Thompson vs. George Robinson.* On January 6, 1864 Thompson filed suit against Robinson for the compensation in the   commission of a tombstone, in memory of Robinson's wife, Martha.

Thompson had sent a proposal to Robinson via James Scott as to the two styles of monuments he could produce. Robinson selected the large one and agreed to the price of $250. Robinson gave Scott a $115 down payment which was relayed back to Thompson. It was agreed that the monument be completed by August 1, 1863. Delays occurred as Robinson provided an illegible inscription. Asa Adams, a teamster and neighbor of Robinson's, came to Susanville to pick up the monument in August only to find that it was not finished. When the tombstone was ready for delivery on November 1, 1863 Robinson refused to accept or pay for it, which brought the dispute to court.

A trial was held on January 11, 1864 and Thompson was awarded the balance due of $135, plus the cost of the suit which amounted to $65. An attachment was undertaken in which a lien was placed on Robinson's Willow Ranch. Robinson finally paid and the tombstone was delivered and set. Of final note the death of not only Robinson's wife Martha in 1863, but also of his two children Anna Nora in 1862 and George E. R. in 1863 were the first burials which constituted the founding of the Long Valley Cemetery in Doyle, 45 miles southeast of Susanville.

And finally, during the 1860s there were two beer breweries operating in Susanville. While sorting through the court documents for cataloging, there was an odd document, among the papers, and though it is not court related, it is of interest.

BREWERS SOLILOQUY
Confound that Taylor! I wish the glib tongue of his had stuck to the roof of his mouth before he ever found his way to Susanville. Before his arrival in town I was selling from sixty to eighty gallons of beer per week. Now my total sales are hardly ten. Encouraged by past success I had laid in a large stock of ingredients which will be almost a total loss. Let me see -- Barley ten thousand pounds -

two hundred dollars is worth now but one hundred fifty - fifty lost there. Twenty old pairs of gum boots and fifteen old horse blankets for flavor - cost twenty dollars - total loss. Heads, horns and hides from slaughter yard for filtering purposes - twenty dollars - total loss - other offals to given tone to yeast twenty five dollars thrown away. Trade gone - brewery almost worthless. Oh dear Oh! Confound Taylor and the Good Templars.

Author unknown
circa 1866

VIII. MEMBERS OF THE BAR
AND BENCH

These brief accounts are centered towards the individuals and their roles with the legal system.

Cutler Arnold (1820-1893) was a resident of the Honey Lake Valley from 1857 to 1868. He served as Plumas County Justice of the Peace, Honey Lake Township from December 1861 to October 1862. His only association with the legal profession was during his residency in the Valley. In the year 1857 Arnold is credited with the construction and operation of Susanville's first hotel.

Valentine John Borrette (1824-1913) served as the first Justice of the Peace of Honey Lake Township, Plumas County, California. He was elected on November 6, 1860 and opened the court docket on November 25, 1860 and served in that capacity until December 1861. Borrette's 235-page docket was used by his successors until it was filled in January 1864. After Borrette's tenure as a Plumas County official, in 1862 he was elected Clerk of Roop County. Borrette left the region in 1870, first moving to Nevada and then to Washington state. He returned to Susanville in 1902 and died there in 1913.

Zenas J. Brown (1812-1895) was admitted to the bar in July 1862 for Lake County, Nevada Territory after successfully passing the examination given by Judge Mott. He was elected as Justice of the Peace on September 3, 1862 for Lassen Township, Lake County, Nevada Territory. While Brown never presided over Court, there were deeds that he certified in this position. Brown, who was also a druggist, received the nickname of Dr. Eight Square, when in 1860 he constructed an octagonal building in Susanville. In the formation process of the County of Lassen, Brown was appointed County Coroner but failed to qualify. In the fall of 1864 Brown sold out his holdings, which consisted of the Susanville's first addition known as Brown Town. Brown moved to various locations and died at La Mesa, California in 1895.

John R. Buckbee (died 1873), was admitted to practice law in Plumas County, California in June 1854 where he maintained a law office in Quincy. For a brief time he was associated with John S. Ward and handled many cases in the Honey Lake Valley. Buckbee was quite active in politics and in 1867 he was elected to the California State

Assembly representing both Lassen and Plumas Counties. He played an influential role in the commutation of Richard Thompson's sentence from execution to life in prison. After Buckbee was elected to the Assembly he did not return to this region to practice law.

William R. Harrison (1813-1870) was one of the senior members of the Honey Lake bar and bench. Prior to his arrival in Susanville in 1864, he had served as a County Judge in two neighboring California Counties--Shasta and Tehama--and also served a term as District Attorney of Tehama County. In 1865 Harrison was elected Lassen County District Court Judge and would also preside in Justice Court when the regular Justice was absent. In 1868 Harrison was appointed Lassen County District Attorney and remained in that position until his death in 1870.

John Lambert (unknown) came to Susanville in 1863 and for a brief time he was in partnership with George May. Even though he was elected to the California State Assembly in 1871, little is known about him.

George May (unknown) had a law practice in Susanville from 1863 to 1865 and had a brief association with attorney John Lambert. While there is no background information on him, there is one fact we know about him: that he possessed the best penmanship in the legal community.

Isaac Newton Roop (1822-1869) came to California to assist his brother Josiah who had a general store in the town of Shasta. In 1854 Isaac and another brother Ephraim built a trading post in the Honey Lake Valley along Nobles' Emigrant Trail, which in reality began the formation of the town of Susanville. Roop was extremely active in the early-day political affairs of the Valley and that of the Nevada Territory where he held several offices. Roop left behind an interesting legacy of comments during his career as lawyer, politician, developer, etc. A classic example of Roop's wit can be found in the records pertaining to his bar examination before Judge Gordon Mott. At that hearing a lawyer from Carson City, Nevada attempted to provide some assistance to Roop. The bar examination was fairly simple and one of the more difficult questions was the definition of a corporation. The Carson attorney informed Roop that: "*A corporation is a creature of the law, having certain powers and duties of a natural person.*" When Judge Mott asked Roop to define a corporation, Roop replied, "*A corporation is a band of fellows without any soul, of whom the law is a creature, who have some powers and take a great deal many more, and entirely ignore the statutory duties imposed upon them.*" Thus with that remark, Roop was admitted to practice law in the Nevada Territory. Roop was a frequent visitor in the Justice Court as attorney, plaintiff and defendant. In 1865 Roop was elected Lassen County District Attorney, and was re-elected to the office in 1868 but did not serve the second term as he failed to file a bond to qualify for office. After a brief illness Roop died in Susanville on February 14, 1869.

Ephraim VanBuren Spencer (1836-1904) came to Honey Lake Valley in 1859. His initial occupation was that of a lumberman, but while working as a sawyer he sustained a severe injury to his right shoulder forcing him to abandon that occupation. In 1862 Spencer, along with five other Honey Lakers, passed the Nevada Territory bar examination and began a long career in law, which would span five decades. In 1864 Spencer was elected as Lassen County's first District Attorney and served in that capacity two additional terms during the 1870s. Spencer was recognized as one the foremost criminal lawyers of Northern California. In 1895 he served a term in the California State Assembly. After his duties as Assemblyman were over, he returned to practice law in Susanville until his death in 1904.

John Sherrill Ward (1825-1872) crossed the plains to California in 1855 from his native Vermont. He settled in Honey Lake Valley in 1858 and with his good friend Isaac Roop was instrumental in the formation of Lassen County. Ward was admitted to practice law in Lake County, Nevada Territory in 1862. On January 20, 1863 Judge Gordon Mott swore in Ward as Judge of Roop County, and he later became one of the main instigators who caused the Sagebrush

War. After his appointment as Judge, Ward issued an injunction against William J. Young, the Plumas justice for Honey Lake Township restraining him from exercising any judicial duties in the confines of Roop County. Young carried on with business as usual, even after he was arrested and fined $100 for contempt in the Roop County Court. Two weeks later Plumas County Court Judge E. T. Hogan issued a warrant for the arrest of Ward and during the attempted arrest ignited the one day shoot-out between the Plumas and Roop County officials.

On December 3, 1863 with bright prospects of a new California county being created in the Honey Lake Valley region, Ward qualified at Justice of Peace, Honey Lake Township, Plumas County. Ward held the position for five months, when in May 1864 William Young was elected Judge for the newly created Susanville Township, Lassen County. In 1870 the population of the region had been greatly reduced and Ward lamented that he was the only attorney in Susanville and had to deal with the dilemma of both opposing parties attempting to retain his services. Ward was extremely active in the civil affairs of the region, went to Washington, D.C. to procure a Government Land Office for Susanville which was granted in 1871 and he served as its first Registrar. His sudden death the next year came as a shock to the community. He lies in an unmarked grave in the Susanville Cemetery.

William J. Young (unknown) presided as Justice of Peace for both Lassen and Plumas County jurisdictions from October 1862 to October 18, 1865. His court was an extremely busy one due in part to the area's flourishing economy, which would rapidly decline by the mid 1860s. In 1862 Young opened the area's first photography gallery. After his tenure as Judge, Young moved to parts unknown.

APPENDIX

JUSTICE COURT - PLAINTIFF'S INDEX

Case Numbers. Please note that the compiler of this work arbitrarily assigned the case number to these cases for indexing purposes, as the court never assigned case numbers. JC refers to a folio file while JD refers to the Justice Court Docket.

Case #	Plaintiff	Defendant	Year
JC 27	A. Evans & Bro.	Disabell, J.H.	1866
JC 222	Adams, Abijah	Swearinger, S	1864
JC 478	Adams, Abijah	Tunnell, S.P.	1867
JC 121	Adams, Asa	Coulthurst, I	1862
JC 48	Adams, Bige	Mulkey, C.	1865
JC 184	Adams, Chas.	Ensley, A.	1864
JC 192	Adams, Chas.	Spencer, E	1864
JC 413	Adams, Henry E.	Findley, Simpson	1864
JD 7	Arnold, Emily	Holcomb, A.A.	1861
JC 88	Asher, M.	Miller, JC	1865
JC 406	Asher, M. & Co.	Perkins, J.R.	1866
JD 15	Atchison, George	Hall, Wright P.	1861
JC 158	Bagin, P.	Riley, C.	1863
JC 161	Bagin, P.	Jackman, -	1863
JC 186	Bangham, E.G.	Ensley, A.	1864
JD 12	Bare, Thomas	White, W.	1861
JC 148	Barker, W.	Mathews, G.F.	1863
JC 196	Barnes, AH	Douglas, R.E.	1864
JC 84	Barnes, Truman	Thompson, M.	1864
JC 237	Barton, Frank	Moody, R.F.	1867
JC 107	Bates, H.	Vaden, E.	1867
JC 367	Bates, H.P.	Writ of Habeas	1868
JC 226	Biddle, J.	Mulkey, C.	1864
JC 38	Biddle, John	Sovy, E.C.	1865
JC 163	Bidwell, H.C.	Bass et al	1863
JC 438	Borrette, H.S.	Haviland, Mark	1863
JC 430	Borrette, V.J.	Kingsbury et al	1864
JC 17	Bowman, E.D.	Lathrop, G.	1866
JC 234	Bowman & Sneath	Roop et al	1868
JC 450	Bowman & Sneath	Stockton, et al	1864

Case #	Plaintiff	Defendant	Year
JC 174	Braden, H	Brunty, --	1864
JD 28	Brannon & Giddings	Nichols, et al	1863
JC 255	Brannon, E.	Thompson, U	1862
JC 247	Brannon, E.	Brewster, H	1863
JC 253	Brannon, E.	Johnson, F.	1864
JC 257	Brannon, E.	Boody, J	1863
JC 356	Brannon, E.	Robertson, Benj.	1865
JD 4	Brannon, E.	Rugg, C.E.	1861
JC 22	Brashear, W.	Reed, A.	1866
JC 152	Brashear et al	Dakin, A.	1863
JC 154	Brashear et al	Patterson, C.	1863
JC 376	Breed & Bro.	Nelson, A.H.	1864
JC 77	Breed, L.	Swearinger, S	1864
JC 4	Brockman, W.	Perkins, J.	1866
JD 29	Bryant, D.W.	Miller, J.C.	1863
JC 128	Burkett, J.	Hume, M.	1862
JC 137	Burkett, J.	Porter, M.	1863
JC 442	Burkett, John	Parker, E.D.	1862
JC 240	Burroughs, D.	Ewings, J.	1865
JC 399	Burt & Tipton	Blake & Williams	1867
JC 453	Byers, James D.	Swearinger, Samuel	1865
Jc 431	Byrd, John	James, G.W.	1863
JC 103	Campbell, W.A.	Gray, A.	1865
JC 414	Chamberlin, P.	Adams, Henry E.	1864
JC 10	Chapman et al	Donaldson, L	1866
JC 160	Clark, A.B.	Leroy, A.	1863
JC 213	Clark, C.B.	Thayer, G.	1864
JC 26	Clark et al	Rice et al	1866
JC 187	Clark et al	Miller et al	1864
JC 16	Clemmons et al	Mulkey, C.	1866
JC 21	Clemmons et al	Miller, W	1866
JC 100	Clemmons et al	Pine, J	1865
JC 114	Clemmons et al	Vance, E.	1867
JC 45	Clemmons, WW	Walker, G.	1865
JC 477	Coburn, John	Smith & Seaman	1864
JC 9	Coleman, J	Howard, S.	1866
JC 145	Cornelison, W.	Miller, J	1863
JC 198	Cornelison, W	Hostetter, F.	1864

Case #	Plaintiff	Defendant	Year
JC 199	Cornelison, W.	Hostetter, F.	1864
JC 230	Cornell & Hamilton	Vincent, Dow	1864
JC 407	Cornell & Hamilton	Lyon, George	1866
JC 15	Corvalis, Benton	Hough, Levi	1866
JC 138	Cowen, J.H.	Brewster, H.	1863
JC 219	Cowen, J.H.	Miller, Wm.	1864
JC 254	Cowen, J.H.	Brannon, E.	1862
JC 389	Cragin, Milo	Housen, -----	1863
JC 86	Cunningham, N.C.	Davis, N.	1864
JC 135	Dake, C.W.	Thompson, H.F.	1863
JC 239	Dakin, H.H.	Elliott & Lwers	1865
JC 259	Davidson, Wilson	Rooks, Wm.	1863
JC 156	Davis, J.F.	McCarger & Co.	1863
JC 143	Davis, S.	Swearinger,	1863
JC 387	Davis, S.	Thompson, H.F.	1863
JC 443	Davis, S.W.	Holcomb, A.A.	1863
JC 25	Dillon, A.	Storff, A.	1866
JC 99	Dobyns & Eldred	Hardesty, J	1865
JC 73	Drake & Pierce	Conkey, S.	1864
JC 131	Drake & Pierce	Elliott, W.T.C.	1862
JC 206	Drake & Spencer	Cables, John	1864
JD 22	Drake, Frank	Elliott, W.T.C.	1862
JC 13	Earls, W.A.	Collins, John	1866
JC 99	Eldred & Dobyns	Hardesty, J.	1865
JC 18	Elliott, W.T.C.	Reed, A. & Bro.	1866
JC 476	Emerson, B.F.	Dakin & Spalding	1865
JC 108	Emerson, C.T.	LeeRoy, A.R.	1867
JC 177	Fitzgerald, Easom	Peyser, S.	1864
JD 18	Fleming, Alexander	Adams, Charles	1861
JC 256	Ford, Johnson P.	Brannon & Giddings	1863
JC 204	Ford, William	Huling & Westfall	1864
JD 16	Fredonyer, A.	Affidavit	1861
JC 37	Giddings, C.	Waterland, W.	1865
JC 150	Giddings, C.	Thompson, H.F.	1863
JC 170	Giddings, Czar	Straus, G.	1864

Case #	Plaintiff	Defendant	Year
JC 371	Goldstein & Co.	Adams, Henry	1864
JC 359	Grey, Geo. W.	Asher, M.	1867
JC 230	Hamilton & Cornell	Vincent, Dow	1864
JC 407	Hamilton & Cornell	Lyon, George	1866
JC 49	Hamilton & Spencer	McCarger & Gibson	1865
JC 202	Hardin, A.W.	Wedekind, Geo. L.	1864
JC 408	Harris, E.W.	Hough, Levi	1867
JC 14	Harris, Jackson	Tyrell, Henry	1866
	Harvey & Hosselkus	see Hosselkus & Harvey	
JC 207	Hauff, Earnest	Burr, Wm.	1864
JD 3	Haviland, M.W.	Shearer Bros.	1861
JC 23	Heap, George P.	Elledge, A.D.	1866
JD 11	Hildreth, E.	Fraiser, -----	1861
JC 218	Hill, Wm. R.	Brown, Z.J.	1864
JC 42	Hines, Fred	Wilmans & Stinson	1865
JC 129	Hollingsworth, J.	Holcomb, A.A.	1862
JC 51	Hosselkus & Harvey	Cowan, J.H.	1865
JC 63	Hosselkus & Harvey	Thompson, et al	1865
JC 164	Hosselkus & Harvey	Holmes & Jones	1863
JC 165	Hosselkus & Harvey	Judkins, A.B.	1863
JC 188	Hosselkus & Harvey	Roop, I & E	1864
JC 189	Hosselkus & Harvey	Goior, Louis	1864
JC 193	Hosselkus & Harvey	Wilmans, D.I.	1864
JC 224	Hosselkus & Harvey	Cheney, E.M.	1864
JC 250	Hosselkus & Harvey	Naliegh, Wm. H.	1863
JC 472	Hosselkus & Harvey	Hardin, A.W.	1865
JC 134	Hosselkus, E.D.	Thompson, H.F.	1863
JD 37	Hosselkus, E.D.	Naileigh, W.H.	1863
JC 133	Howe, J.W.M.	McCoulloch, W.	1867
JC 200	Howe, J.W.M.	Preble, -----	1864
JC 216	Howe, J.W.M.	Doe, John	1864
JC 233	Howe, John	Burk, Thomas	1864
JC 203	Hundley, P.O.	Spencer, et al	1864
JD 21	Huntington, James	Moffat, Joshua	1862
JC 71	Imer, Peter	Coulthurst, Isaac	1865
JC 185	James, Preston	Lockman, Warren	1864

Case #	Plaintiff	Defendant	Year
JD 9	Jenkins, L.T.	Reppert, A.	1861
JC 110	Johnson, O.N.	Vance, G.W. et al	1867
JC 98	Johnston, Robert	Purcell, George	1865
JC 400	Kelley, George F.	Holland, et al	1867
JC 448	Kelley, George F.	Moody, R.F.	1865
JC 67	Kingsbury & Co.	Idaho-CA Stage Co.	1865
JD 23	Kingsbury, W.C.	Burkett, John	1862
	Kingsley & Miller	See Miller & Kingsley	
JC 455	Kingsley & Watson	Hardesty, Wm.	1865
JC 117	Knoch, D.	Page, J.	1867
JC 119	Knoch, D.	Spencer, E.V.	1868
JC 403	Kobler, John	Straus, Joseph	1865
JC 32	Kyle, C.A.	Vincent, Dow	1865
JD 26	Lake, M.C.	Winchel & Kelley	1863
JC 11	Laird, Sarah T.	Holmes, Jasper	1866
JC 401	Lander, Boson	Teft, Hiram	1864
JC 480	Lattin, Samuel	Wiggin, J.M.	1866
JC 53	Leroy, A.R.	Swearinger, Sam	1865
JC 457	Leroy, A.R.	Harold, Richard	1864
JD 19	Logan, William	Hill, Smith J.	1862
JC 151	Long & Leroy	Thompson, H.F.	1863
JC 179	Long & Leroy	Purdom, T.C.	1864
JC 149	Long, Henry	Moffatt, Joshua	1863
JC 358	Long, Henry	Kingsbury, W.V.	1865
JC 69	Longmore, A.C.	Hardesty, Wm.	1865
JC 106	M. Asher & Co.	Gray, G.W.	1867
JC 52	M. Heller & Bro.	Goldstien & Jacobs	1865
JC 76	Manning, J.P.	Mellis, John	1864
JD 13	Marriott, J.	Robinson, John	1861
JC 245	Mathews, E.F.	Doe, John	1863
JC 197	May, George	Shaddock, John	1864
JC 205	May, George	Hoover, William	1864
JC 446	May, George	Bass, E.	1864
JC 87	McDermit, M.	Smith & Clarkin	1865
JC 102	Miller & Kingsley	Pine & Chapman	1865
JC 157	Miller & Kingsley	Clark, A.B.	1863

Case #	Plaintiff	Defendant	Year
JC 180	Miller & Kingsley	Peters, J.C.	1864
JC 182	Miller & Kingsley	Peters & Cockran	1864
JC 215	Miller & Kingsley	Biddle, John	1864
JC 228	Miller & Kingsley	Stockton, H.C.	1864
JC 454	Miller & Kingsley	Long & Leroy	1865
JC 87	Miller, G.G.	Hostetter, F.M.	1864
JC 191	Miller, Wm. T.	Goiore, Louis	1864
JC 19	Naliegh, W.H.	Pine & Chapman	1866
JC 85	Neale, A.C.	Adams, Asa	1864
JC 225	Neale, A.C.	Adams, Henry E.	1864
JC 402	Neale, John H.	Giddings, Czar	1865
JC 178	Nelson, A.H.	Wedekind, George L.	1864
JC 181	Nelson, A.H.	Deeds, James	1864
JD 8	Nichols, E.R.	Weatherlow, Wm.	1861
JC 101	P.W. Cunningham & Co.	Pine, J.N.	1865
JD 6	Parker, James	Sanborn, et al	1861
JC 208	Parker, John	Reppert, H.H. et al	1864
	People of the State	See Defendant's index	
JC 167	Perry, George W.	Winchell & Kelley	1863
JC 80	Peyser, S.	Findley, Ebenezer	1864
JC 183	Peyser, S.	Wedekind, Geo.	1864
JC 252	Peyser, S.	Brannon, E.	1864
JD 25	Philips, N.	Holden, Thos.	1863
JC 470	Pickard, John	Miller, G.G. & Bro.	1863
JC 82	Pickard, Thomas W.	Spatta, Gabriel	1864
JC 398	Pickard, Thomas W.	Adams, Asa	1864
JC 479	Pierce, T.R.	Kelley, C.M.	1869
JC 59	Pine, J.N.	Kerns, N.	1865
JC 139	Pond, E.B.	Williams, Frank et al	1863
JC 28	Preble & Stark	Ramsey, A.	1866
JC 29	Preble, L. F.	Rice, E.	1866
JC 220	Preble, L.F.	Stockton, H.C.	1864
JC 368	Preble, L.F.	Brannon, E.	1865
JC 176	Pyror, Miller	Reavis, Andrew	1864
JC 195	Purdom, T.C.	Wilmans, D.I.	1864

Case #	Plaintiff	Defendant	Year
JC 212	Ramsey, A.	Lanigar, F.	1864
JC 168	Rayman, M.	Phillips, N.	1864
JC 79	Read, Samuel	Meharry, John	1864
JC 474	Reppert Bros.	Haley & Malone	1871
JC 132	Reyman, M.	Phillips, N.	1863
JC 130	Rice, Edward	Priddy, Morris	1862
JC 62	Robertson, Benj. J.	Brannon, Emanuel	1865
JC 251	Robertson, Benj. J.	Sovey, E.C.	1865
JC 169	Robinson, Geo.	Adams & Scott	1864
JC 471	Robinson, Thomas	Mulroney & Lieth	1864
JC 140	Roop, Isaac	Alvord, C.E.	1863
JC 390	Roop, Isaac N.	Dake, C.W.	1864
JC 392	Roop, Isaac N.	Teft, H.	1864
JC 394	Roop, Isaac N.	Wentworth, Wm.	1863
JC 464	Roop, Isaac N.	Long, T.N.	1864
JD 27	Roop, Isaac N.	Seaman, -----	1863
JD 36	Sain, H.	Jackman, -----	1863
JC 223	Sanders, W.	Wright, A.D.	1864
JC 172	Seaman, A.	Hough, Levi	1864
JC 459	Seaman, Aaron	Packard, ----	1864
JC 469	Skadan, H.N.	Riley, Henry	1866
JC 125	Slater, John A.	Varney, E.L.	1862
JC 118	Sloss, F.A.	Wentworth, Wm.	1867
JC 1	Smith, A.A.	Townsend, E.	1866
JC 12	Smith, A.A.	Lyon, George	1866
JC 136	Smith, Samuel	Emerson, Chas.	1863
JC 201	Smith, William	Dake, C.W.	1864
JC 450	Sneath & Bowman	Stockton & Andrews	1864
JC 241	Soule, E.P.	Elliott & Lewers	1865
JC 46	Southworth. L.	Wilmans, D.I.	1865
JC 445	Southworth, L.	Miller, J. & Bro.	1865
JC 331	Sovy, E.C.	Biddle, John	1865
JC 70	Spargur, H.L.	Clark, James H.	1865
JC 206	Spencer & Drake	Cables, John	1864
JC 68	Spencer, E.V.	Idaho & CA Stage	1865
JC 78	Spencer, E.V.	Swearinger, Sam	1864
JD 1	Spencer, E.V. & Co.	Shearer Bros.	1860
JC 66	Stein, Mrs. R.	Peyser, S.	1865

Case #	Plaintiff	Defendant	Year
JC 133	Stine, George	Peyser & Beanstock	1863
JC 142	Stinson, S.	Wales, Philip	1863
JC 55	Stockton, H.C.	Cowan, J.H.	1865
JC 81	Stockton, H.C.	Jenkerson, Wm.	1864
JC 97	Stockton, H.C.	Pine, J.N.	1865
JC 155	Stockton, H.C.	Judkins, A.B.	1863
JC 214	Stockton, H.C.	Shelley, Wm.	1864
JC 61	Storff, Antone	Olover, Wm.	1865
JD 2	Storff, Antone	Marriott, Samuel	1861
JD 14	Storff, Antone	Tucker, John	1861
JC 105	Strong, Frank S.	Lyon, George	1867
JC 2	Susanville Fire Co.	Ward, John S.	1866
JC 147	Sweet, O.C.	Davis, -------	1863
JC 35	Tarrant, H.F.	Long & Leroy	1865
JC 44	Tarrant, H.F.	Hart, Wm.	1865
JC 385	Taylor, Jarvis	Writ of Habeas C.	1866
JC 461	Thompson, H.F.	Robinson, Geo.	1864
JC 126	Titherington, David	Borette, Fred	1862
JC 399	Tipton & Burt	Blake & Williams	1867
JC 242	Todd, Edward	Tyler, Jerry	1866
JC 123	Towell, Thomas	Haris aka Rocky	1862
JC 162	Towell, Thomas	Jackman, -----	1863
JD 32	Towell, Thomas	Retherford, F.	1863
JC 415	Turnboo, T.H.	Knight, J.	1867
JC 456	Tuttle, Cephus	Cunningham et al	1864
JC 210	Tyler, J.C.	Boyd, A.	1864
JC 481	Vary, L.	Elliott, W.T.C.	1867
JC 120	Varney, E.L.	Long, F.	1862
JC 412	Vincent, Dow	Frost, E.	1864
JC 433	Vincent, Dow	Frost, E.	1864
JC 104	Ward, John S.	Inman, Joseph	1865
JC 370	Ward, John S.	Webb, John	1862
JC 159	Warner, John	Leroy, A.R.	1863
JC 455	Watson & Kingsley	Hardesty, Wm.	1865
JC 395	Weatherlow, Wm.	Marks, L.	1864
JC 122	Webb, John	Alvord, Chas. E.	1862

Case #	Plaintiff	Defendant	Year
JC 404	Wentworth, Wm.	Giddings, Czar	1865
JC 437	Wentworth, Wm.	Wilson, T.C.	1864
JC 458	White, Charles	Stiles, L.C.	1865
JC 391	White, M.G.	Idaho-CA Stage Co.	1867
JC 432	Whiting, L.P.	Dillon & Storff	1867
JC 468	Whiting, L.P.	McNaughton & Bro.	1865
JC 473	Whiting, L.P.	Montgomery, T.	1866
JC 83	Wick, Moses	Sawyer, Lewis A.	1864
JC 30	Wilcox, H.K.	Grey, Pat	1866
JC 230	Williams, John A.	Wedekind, John	1864
JC 231	Williams, Jno.	Cheney, E.M.	1864
JC 354	Williams, Jno.	Conkey, S.	1864
JC 6	Whiting, L.P.	Giddings, C.	1866
JC 20	Whiting, L.P.	Pine & Chapman	1866
JC 146	Whiting, L.P.	Doyle, James	1863
JC 238	Whiting, L.P.	Elliott & Lewers	1864
JC 444	Worm, A.W.	Dake, C.W.	1864
JC 209	Yee, Ah	Henry, Chew	1864

JUSTICE COURT - DEFENDANT'S INDEX

Case #	Defendant	Plaintiff	Year
JC 85	Adams, Asa	Neale, A.C.	1864
JC 398	Adams, Asa	Pickard, Thomas W.	1864
JC 420	Adams, Asa	People of the State	1862
JC 169	Adams, Asa et al	Robinson, Geo.	1864
JD 18	Adams, Charles	Fleming, A.	1861
JC 225	Adams, Henry E.	Neale, A.C.	1864
JC 371	Adams, Henry E.	Goldstien & Co.	1864
JC 414	Adams, Henry E.	Chamberlin, P.	1864
JC 34	Ah, Yee	People of the State	1865
JC 140	Alvord, Chas. E.	Roop, I.N.	1863
JC 122	Alvord, Chas. E.	Webb, John	1862
JC 486	Anderson, John	People of the State	1865
JC 450	Andrews & Stockton	Sneath & Bowman	1864
JC 381	Arnold, H.E.	People of the State	1865
JC 109	Asher, M.	People of the State	1867
JC 359	Asher, M.	Grey, Geo. W.	1867
JC 41	Baker, Joseph	People of the State	1865
JD 6	Banker, John et al	Parker, James	1861
JC 171	Bare, Thomas	People of the State	1864
JC 111	Barnes, Truman et al	People of the State	1867
JC 334	Bartell, George	People of the State	1867
JC 446	Bass, E.	May, George	1864
JC 163	Bass, Ed et al	Bidwell, H.C.	1863
JC 236	Bates, H.P. et al	People of the State	1868
JC 337	Bates, H.P.	People of the State	1867
JC 133	Beanstock & Peyser	Stine, George	1863
JC 374	Beanstock & Peyser	People of the State	1868
JC 430	Belk, W.K. et al	Borrette, V.J.	1864
JC 236	Benjamin, ---- et al	People of the State	1868
JC 215	Biddle, John	Miller & Kingsley	1864
JC 331	Biddle, John	Sovy, E.C.	1865
JC 399	Blake & Williams	Tipton & Burt	1867
JC 463	Blake, John et al	People of the State	1866
JC 127	Blanchard, David	People of the State	1862
JC 257	Boody, Jacob	Brannon & Giddings	1863
JC 126	Borette, Fred	Titherington, David	1862
JC 416	Borrette, H.	People of the State	1865

Case #	Defendant	Plaintiff	Year
JC 139	Bostwick, Newton et al	Pond, E.B.	1863
JC 210	Boyd, A.	Tyler, J.C.	1864
JC 424	Bradley, John	People of the State	1865
JC 368	Brannon, E.	Preble, L.F.	1865
JC 482	Brannon, E.	People of the State	1865
JC 62	Brannon, Emanuel	Robertson, Benj.	1865
JC 252	Brannon, Emanuel	Peyser, S.	1864
JC 254	Brannon, Emanuel	Cowen, J.H.	1862
JC 256	Brannon & Giddings	Ford, Johnson P.	1863
JC 175	Bronson, -----	People of the State	1864
JC 349	Breed, J.H.	People of the State	1864
JC 138	Brewster, Horace	Cowen, J.H.	1863
JC 247	Brewster, Horace	Brannon & Giddings	1863
JC 218	Brown, Z.J.	Hill, Wm. R.	1864
JC 174	Brunty, -----	Bradon, H.N.	1864
JC 233	Burk, Thomas	Howe, J.W.M.	1864
JD 23	Burkett, John	Kingsbury, W.C.	1862
JC 207	Burr, Wm.	Hauff, Earnest	1864
JC 340	Bush, E.	People of the State	1865
JC 350	Byrd, John	People of the State	1864
JC 206	Cables, John	Spencer & Drake	1864
JC 422	Cavenaugh, William	People of the State	1865
JC 19	Chapman, A.F. et al	Naliegh, W.H.	1866
JC 20	Chapman, A.F. et al	Whiting, L.P.	1866
JC 102	Chapman & Pine	Miller & Kingsley	1865
JC 224	Cheney, E.M.	Hosselkus & Harvey	1864
JC 231	Cheney, E.M.	Williams, Jno.	1864
JC 112	China Charley	People of the State	1867
JC 65	China Lem	People of the State	1865
JC 217	Childers, Spencer	People of the State	1864
JC 157	Clark, A.B.	Miller & Kingsley	1863
JC 339	Clark, Jacob	People of the State	1867
JC 70	Clark, James H.	Spargur, H.L.	1865
JC 54	Clarkin, O.W. et al	McDermit, M.	1865
JC 182	Cockran, Jas. et al	Miller & Kingsley	1864
JC 13	Collins, John	Earls, W.A.	1866
JC 429	Collins, John	People of the State	1865

Case #	Defendant	Plaintiff	Year
JC 73	Conkey, S.	Drake & Pierce	1864
JC 354	Conkey, S.	Williams, Jno.	1864
JC 430	Corse, Wm. et al	Borrette, V.J.	1864
JC 425	Corse, Wm. et al	People of the State	1865
JC 71	Coulthurst, Isaac	Imer, Peter	1865
JC 121	Coulthurst, Isaac	Adams, Asa	1862
JC 467	Coulthurst, Isaac	People of the State	1865
JC 51	Cowan, J.H.	Hosselkus & Harvey	1865
JC 55	Cowan, J.H.	Stockton, H.C.	1865
JC 440	Crane, W.H.	People of the State	1865
JC 456	Cunningham, P.W. et al	Tuttle, Cephus	1864
JC 373	Dailey, John et al	People of the State	1867
JC 201	Dake, C.W.	Smith, Wm.	1864
JC 390	Dake, C.W.	Roop, I.N.	1864
JC 444	Dake, C.W.	Worm, A.W.	1864
JC 476	Dakin & Spalding	Emerson, B.F.	1865
JC 152	Dakin, William	Briggs, R. et al	1863
JC 147	Davis, -----	Sweet, O.C.	1863
JC 467	Davis, J. H.	People of the State	1865
JC 86	Davis, Nathaniel	Cunningham, N.C.	1864
JC 181	Deeds, James	Nelson, A.H.	1864
JC 24	Dillon, A.	People of the State	1866
JC 432	Dillon, A. et al	Whiting, L. P.	1867
JC 27	Disabell, A.H.	A. Evans & Bro.	1866
JC 245	Doe, John	Mathews, E.F.	1863
JC 216	Doe, John	Howe, J.W.M.	1864
JC 10	Donaldson, Lewis	Sloss & Chapman	1866
JC 196	Douglas, R.F.	Barnes, A.H.	1864
JC 227	Downing, Andrew et al of the State	People 1864	
JC 144	Doyle, James	People of the State	1863
JC 146	Doyle, James	Whiting, L.P.	1863
JC 23	Elledge, A.D.	Heap, George P.	1866
JC 131	Elliott, W.T.C.	Drake & Pierce	1862
JC 481	Elliott, W.T.C.	Vary, L.	1867
JD 22	Elliott, W.T.C.	Drake, Frank	1862

Case #	Defendant	Plaintiff	Year
JC 238	Elliott, W.T.C. et al	Whiting, L.P.	1864
JC 239	Elliott, W.T.C. et al	Dakin, Hiram H.	1865
JC 241	Elliott, W.T.C. et al	Soule, E.P.	1865
JC 93	Emerson, C.T.	People of the State	1865
JC 136	Emerson, Chas.	Smith, Samuel	1863
JC 184	Ensley, A.	Adams, Chas.	1864
JC 186	Ensley, Allen	Bangham, E.G.	1864
JC 240	Ewings, Joseph	Burroughs, D.	1865
JC 378	Evans, A.	People of the State	1864
JC 413	Findley, Simpson	Adams, Henry E.	1864
JC 465	Flynn, Thos. et al	People of the State	1866
JD 11	Frasier, -----	Hildreth, E.	1861
JD 16	Fredonyer, Atlas	Affidavit	1861
JC 153	Friedman, S.	People of the State	1863
JC 412	Frost, E.	Vincent, Dow	1864
JC 433	Frost, E.	Vincent, Dow	1864
JC 115	Fry, C.D.	People of the State	1867
JC 352	Galt, J.	People of the State	1867
JC 49	Gibson, S. et al	Hamilton & Spencer	1865
JC 6	Giddings, C.	Whiting, L.P.	1866
JC 5	Giddings, C.	People of the State	1866
JC 404	Giddings, C.	Wentworth, Wm.	1865
JC 402	Giddings, C.	Neale, John H.	1865
JC 256	Giddings, C. et al	Ford, Johnson P.	1863
JC 189	Goior, Louis	Hosselkus & Harvey	1864
JC 191	Goior, Louis	Miller, Wm. T.	1864
JC 52	Goldstein, E. et al	M. Heller & Bro.	1865
JC 57	Goldstein, E.	People of the State	1865
JC 26	Goos, A. William et al	Clark & Hamilton	1866
JC 379	Gossage, J.	People of the State	1865
JC 103	Gray, A.	Campbell, W.A.	1865
JC 106	Gray, G.W. et al	M. Asher & Co.	1867
JC 208	Grenile, Lafayette et al	Parker, John et al	1866
JC 30	Grey, Pat	Wilcox, H.K.	1866

Case #	Defendant	Plaintiff	Year
JC 441	Hager, J.F.	People of the State	1865
JC 56	Haley, J.	People of the State	1865
JC 348	Hall, S.	People of the State	1864
JC 343	Hall, S.R.	People of the State	1865
JD 15	Hall, Wright P.	Atchison, George	1861
JC 485	Harbin, J.H.	People of the State	1865
JC 99	Hardesty, Jacob	Dobyns & Eldred	1865
JC 69	Hardesty, William	Longmore, A.C.	1865
JC 455	Hardesty, William	Watson & Kingsley	1865
JC 94	Hardin, A.H.	People of the State	1865
JC 472	Hardin, A.H.	Hosselkus & Harvey	1865
JC 123	Haris J.P.	Towell, Thomas	1862
JC 483	Haris, J.P.	People of the State	1862
JC 457	Harold, Richard	Leroy, A.R.	1864
JC 405	Harris, Jackson	People of the State	1865
JC 44	Hart, Wm.	Tarrant, H.F.	1865
JC 342	Harvey, I.J.	People of the State	1865
JC 438	Haviland, Mark	Borrette, H.S.	1863
JC 72	Heap, George P.	People of the State	1865
JC 209	Henry, Chew	Yee, Ah	1864
JC 106	Hickerson, ------	M. Asher & Co.	1867
JC 389	Hill, Smith J.	People of the State	1869
JD 19	Hill, Smith J.	Logan, William	1862
JC 129	Holcomb, A.A.	Hollingsworth, J.	1862
JC 443	Holcomb, A.A.	Davis, S.W.	1863
JD 7	Holcomb, A.A.	Arnold, Emily	1861
JC 380	Holcomb, J.J.	People of the State	1865
JD 25	Holden, Thomas	Philips, N.	1863
JC 400	Holland, James et al	Kelley, George F.	1867
JC 421	Holliday, -----	People of the State	1865
JC 164	Holmes & Jones	Hosselkus & Harvey	1863
JC 11	Holmes, Jasper	Laird, Sarah T.	1866
JC 205	Hoover, William	May, George	1864
JC 199	Hostetter, F.M.	Cornelison, Wiley	1864
JC 198	Hostetter, F.M.	Cornelison, Wiley	1864
JC 15	Hough, Levi	Corvalis, Benton	1866
JC 172	Hough, Levi	Seaman, A.	1864
JC 408	Hough, Levi	Harris, E.W.	1867
JC 389	Housin, -----	Cragin, Milo	1863

Case #	Defendant	Plaintiff	Year
JC 9	Howard, S.D.	Coleman, J.E.	1866
JC 89	Huff, J.B.	People of the State	1865
JC 204	Huling, Edwin et al	Ford, William	1864
JC 128	Hume, Mr.	Burkett, John	1862
JD 28	Huntington, James et al	Brannon & Giddings	1863
JC 249	Hyde, George	People of the State	1862
JC 67	Idaho & Calif. Stage Co.	Kinsgbury & Co.	1865
JC 68	Idaho & Calif. Stage Co.	Spencer, E.V.	1865
JC 391	Idaho & Calif. Stage Co.	White, M.G.	1867
JC 104	Inman, Joseph	Ward, John S.	1865
JC 161	Jackman, ------	Bagin, P.	1863
JC 162	Jackman, ------	Towell, Thomas	1863
JD 36	Jackman, ------	Sain, H.	1863
JC 52	Jacobs, L. et al	M. Heller & Bro.	1865
JC 344	Jacobs, Lew	People of the State	1865
JC 431	James, G.W.	Byrd, John	1863
JC 386	Jamison, M.M.	People of the State	1865
JC 81	Jenkerson, W.M.	Stockton, H.C.	1864
JC 462	Jenkerson, W.M.	People of the State	1865
JC 253	Johnson, F.	Brannan & Giddings	1864
JC 456	Johnson, F.S.	Tuttle, Cephus	1864
JC 164	Jones & Holmes	Hosselkus & Harvey	1863
JC 382	Jones, Abraham	People of the State	1865
JC 155	Judkins, A.B.	Stockton, H.C.	1863
JC 165	Judkins, A.B.	Hosselkus & Harvey	1863
JD 31	Kearns, N. et al	People of the State	1863
JD 26	Kelley & Winchel	Lake, M.C.	1863
JC 479	Kelley, C.M.	Pierce, T.R.	1869
JC 116	Kelley, J.D.	People of the State	1867
JC 167	Kelley, J.D. et al	Perry, Geo. W.	1863
JC 372	Kelley, Peter	People of the State	1864
JC 59	Kerns, N.	Pine, J.N.	1865

Case #	Defendant	Plaintiff	Year
JC 110	Kingsbury, W.C. et al	Johnson, O.N.	1867
JC 430	Kingsbury, W.C. et al	Borrette, V.J.	1864
JC 425	Kingsbury, W.C. et al	People of the State	1865
JC 358	Kingsbury, W.V.	Long, Henry	1865
JC 415	Knight, J.	Turnboo, T.H.	1867
JC 212	Lanigar, F.	Ramsey, A.	1864
JC 17	Lathrop, George	Bowman, E.D.	1866
JC 435	Lathrop, George	People of the State	1865
JC 112	Lee Sing	People of the State	1867
JC 471	Leith & Mulroney	Robinson, Thos V.	1864
JC 108	LeRoy, A.R.	Emerson, C.T. et al	1867
JC 159	LeRoy, A.R.	Warner, John	1863
JC 160	LeRoy, A.R.	Clark, A.B.	1863
JC 451	Lewis, Robinson	People of the State	1865
JC 185	Lockman, Warren	James, Preston	1864
JC 35	Long & LeRoy	Tarrant, H.F.	1865
JC 454	Long & LeRoy	Miller & Kingsley	1865
JC 120	Long, F.	Varney, E.L.	1862
JC 333	Longmore, A.C.	People of the State	1867
JC 451	Louis, Robinson	People of the State	1865
JD 33	Lowrie, David	People of the State	1863
JC 12	Lyon, George	Smith, A.A.	1866
JC 105	Lyon, George	Strong, Frank S.	1867
JC 407	Lyon, George	Hamilton & Cornell	1866
JC 336	Marks, Lafayette	People of the State	1863
JC 346	Marks, Lafayette	People of the State	1864
JC 7	Marks, Lafayette	People of the State	1866
JC 395	Marks, Lafayette	Weatherlow, Wm.	1864
JC 487	Marks, Lafayette	People of the State	1867
JC 489	Marks, Lafayette	People of the State	1872
JC 490	Marks, Lafayette	People of the State	1875
JC 351	Marriott, Samuel	People of the State	1865
JC 50	Marriott, Samuel	People of the State	1865
JC 95	Marriott, Samuel	People of the State	1865
JD 2	Marriott, Samuel	Storff, Antone	1861
JC 148	Mathews, G.F.	Barker, Wm.	1863
JC 49	McCarger, Alfred		

Case #	Defendant	Plaintiff	Year
	et al	Hamilton & Spencer	1865
JC 357	McCarger, Alfred	People of the State	1863
JC 156	McCarger, Alfred & Co.	Davis, J.F.	1863
JC 113	McCoulloch, William	Howe, J.W.M.	1867
JC 468	McNaughton, S. & Bro.	Whiting, L.P.	1865
JC 76	Mellis, John	Manning, J.P.	1864
JC 79	Meharry, John	Read, Samuel	1864
JC 187	Miller, G.G. et al	Clark & Hamilton	1864
JC 470	Miller, G.G. & Bro.	Pickard, John	1863
JC 310	Miller, Frank	People of the State	1864
JC 190	Miller, Henry et al	People of the State	1864
JC 445	Miller, J. & Bro.	Southworth, L.	1865
JC 88	Miller, J.C.	Asher, Meyer	1865
JC 145	Miller, J.C.	Cornelison, Wiley	1863
JD 29	Miller, J.C.	Byrant, D.W.	1863
JC 78	Miller, J.C. et al	Stark, Lewis	1864
JC 143	Miller, J.C. et al	Davis, S.	1863
JC 187	Miller, John	Clark & Hamilton	1864
JC 75	Miller, R.D.	People of the State	1864
JC 418	Miller, R.D.	People of the State	1865
JC 21	Miller, William	Clemmons & Co.	1866
JC 219	Miller, William	Cowen, J.H.	1864
JC 149	Moffatt, Joshua	Long, Henry	1863
JD 21	Moffatt, Joshua	Huntington, James	1862
JC 74	Montgomery, Thomas	People of the State	1864
JC 353	Montgomery, Thomas	People of the State	1864
JC 396	Montgomery, Thomas	People of the State	1870
JC 397	Montgomery, Thomas	People of the State	1865
JC 449	Montgomery, Thomas	People of the State	1869
JC 473	Montgomery, Thomas	Whiting, L.P.	1866
JC 237	Moody, R.F.	Barton, Frank A.	1867
JC 448	Moody, R.F.	Kelley, George F.	1865
JC 383	Moon, A.G.	People of the State	1867
JD 9	Morrow, J. et al	People of the State	1861
JC 347	Mosier, Fred	People of the State	1864
JC 16	Mulkey, C.	Clemmons & Myers	1866
JC 48	Mulkey, C.	Adams, Bige	1865

Case #	Defendant	Plaintiff	Year
JD 34	Mulkey, C.	People of the State	1863
JC 226	Mulkey, Charles	Biddle, John	1864
JC 471	Mulroney & Lieth	Robinson, Thos.	1864
JC 274	Myers, Barbara	Shearer, Josiah	1887
JC 452	Myers, J.	People of the State	1867
JC 488	Myers, Joseph	People of the State	1867
JC 428	Myers, Martin	People of the State	1865
JC 250	Naileigh, Wm. H.	Hosselkus & Harvey	1863
JC 434	Naileigh, Wm. H.	People of the State	1865
JD 37	Naileigh, Wm H.	Hosselkus, E.D.	1863
JC 63	Naileigh, Wm. H. et al	Hosselkus & Harvey	1865
JC 376	Nelson, A.H.	Breed & Bro.	1864
JC 410	Nelson, A.H.	People of the State	1864
JD 28	Nichols, E.R. et al	Brannan & Giddings	1863
JC 338	Nixon, Chas.	People of the State	1864
JC 436	Oiler, William	People of the State	1865
JC 61	Olover, Wm.	Storff, Antone	1865
JC 459	Packard, -----	Seaman, Aaron	1864
JC 117	Page, J.	Knoch, D.	1867
JC 141	Painter, Benj. B.	People of the State	1863
JC 442	Parker, E.D.	Burkett, John	1862
JC 154	Patterson, Chas.	Briggs, R. et al	1863
JC 332	Peck, O. et al	People of the State	1866
JC 400	Pencole, John et al	Kelley, George F.	1867
JC 406	Perkins, J.R.	M. Asher & Co.	1866
JC 4	Perkins, J.R. & Bro.	Brockman, Wm.	1866
JC 47	Perry, G.W.	People of the State	1865
JC 180	Peters, J.C.	Miller & Kingsley	1864
JC 182	Peters, J.C. et al	Miller & Kingsley	1864
JC 66	Peyser, S.	Stein, Mrs. R.	1865
JC 177	Peyser, S.	Fitzgerald, Easom	1864
JC 133	Peyser & Beanstock	Stine, George	1863
JC 374	Peyser & Beanstock	People of the State	1868
JC 341	Phillips, James	People of the State	1864
JC 132	Phillips, N.	Reyman, M.	1863

Case #	Defendant	Plaintiff	Year
JC 168	Phillips, N.	Rayman, M.	1864
JC 58	Phillips, N.	People of the State	1865
JC 97	Pine, J.N.	Stockton, H. C.	1865
JC 100	Pine, J.N.	Clemmons & Myers	1865
JC 101	Pine, J.N.	Cunningham & Co.	1865
JC 19	Pine, J.N. et al	Naileigh, W.H.	1866
JC 20	Pine, J.N. et al	Whiting, L.P.	1866
JC 137	Porter, M.	Burkett, John	1863
JC 3	Pratt, M.W.	Writ of Habeas C.	1868
JC 235	Pratt, M.W.	People of the State	1868
JC 200	Preble, -----	Howe, J.W.M.	1864
JC 92	Prickett, Jacobs	People of the State	1865
JC 130	Priddy, Morris	Rice, Edward	1862
JC 163	Pritchard, Jno. et al	Bidwell, H.C.	1863
JC 166	Pursell, G.M.	People of the State	1863
JC 98	Pursell, George	Johnston, Robert	1865
JC 179	Purdom, T.C.	Long & Leroy	1864
JC 28	Ramsey, A.	Preble & Stark	1866
JC 227	Rantz, William et al	People of the State	1864
JC 176	Reavis, Andrew	Pyror, Miller	1864
JC 18	Reed, A & Bro.	Elliott, W.T.C.	1866
JC 22	Reed, A & Bro.	Brashear, W.S.	1866
JC 208	Reppert, H.H. et al	Parker, John	1864
JD 10	Reppert, A.	Jenkins, L.T.	1861
JC 173	Retherford, F.	People of the State	1864
JD 32	Retherford, F.	Towell, Thomas	1863
JC 29	Rice, E.	Preble, L.F.	1866
JC 26	Rice, Eli et al	Clark & Hamilton	1866
JC 409	Riddle, William	People of the State	1865
JC 158	Riley, C.	Bagin, P.	1863
JC 469	Riley, Henry	Skadan, H.	1866
JC 373	Riley, Frank et al	People of the State	1867
JC 335	Roach, Amos	People of the State	1864
JC 8	Robertson, B.J.	People of the State	1866
JC 356	Robertson, Benj.	Brannan, E.	1865
JC 461	Robinson, George	Thompson, H.F.	1864
JD 13	Robinson, John	Marriott, J.	1861
JC 123	Rocky aka Haris	Towell, Thomas	1862

Case #	Defendant	Plaintiff	Year
JC 483	Rocky aka Haris	People of the State	1862
JC 259	Rooks, William	Davidson, Wilson	1863
JC 188	Roop, E. et al	Hosselkus & Harvey	1864
JC 188	Roop, I. et al	Hosselkus & Harvey	1864
JC 221	Roop, I.N.	People of the State	1864
JC 393	Roop, I.N.	People of the State	1865
JC 63	Roop, Isaac et al	Hosselkus & Harvey	1865
JC 234	Roop, Isaac et al	Sneath & Bowman	1868
JD 5	Rugg, C.E.	Brannon, E.	1861
JD 9	Rugg, Clark et al	People of the State	1861
JD 6	Sandborn, L. et al	Parker, James	1861
JC 83	Sawyer, Lewis A.	Wick, Moses	1864
JC 169	Scott, Jas. A. et al	Robinson, Geo.	1864
JD 27	Seaman, -----	Roop, I.N.	1863
JC 477	Seaman & Smith	Coburn, John	1864
JC 377	Shackleford, W.A.	People of the State	1865
JC 197	Shaddock, John	May, George	1864
JD 1	Shearer, Jos. & Bro.	Spencer, E.V.	1860
JD 3	Shearer, Jos. & Bro.	Haviland, M.W.	1861
JC 214	Shelley, Wm.	Stockton, H.C.	1864
JC 369	Sherman, C.M.	People of the State	1867
JC 475	Sing, A.	People of the State	1865
JC 477	Smith & Seaman	Coburn, John	1864
JC 54	Smith, Patrick et al	McDermit, M.	1865
JC 251	Sovy, E.C.	Robertson, B.J.	1865
JC 38	Sovy, E.C.	Biddle, John	1865
JC 476	Spalding & Dakin	Emerson, B.F.	1865
JC 60	Spargur, H.L.	People of the State	1865
JC 82	Spatta, Gabriel	Pickard, Thomas W.	1864
JC 119	Spencer, E.V.	Knoch, D.	1868
JC 192	Spencer, E.V.	Adams, Chas.	1864
JC 194	Spencer, E.V.	People of the State	1864
JC 203	Spencer, E.V.	Hundley, P.O.	1864
JD 17	Staig, Dock	People of the State	1861
JC 336	Stencil, -----	People of the State	1863
JC 439	Steward, J.B.	People of the State	1865
JC 458	Stiles, L.C.	White, Charles	1865
JC 42	Stinson, S.S. et al	Hines, Fred	1865

Case #	Defendant	Plaintiff	Year
JC 450	Stockton & Andrews	Sneath & Bowman	1864
JC 220	Stockton, H.C.	Preble, L.F.	1864
JC 228	Stockton, H.C.	Miller & Kingsley	1864
JC 25	Storff, Antone	Dillon, A.	1866
JC 432	Storff, Antone et al	Whiting, L.P.	1867
JC 31	Stout, John et al	People of the State	1863
JC 170	Straus, G.	Giddings, Czar	1864
JC 190	Straus, I. et al	People of the State	1864
JC 243	Straus, Joseph	People of the State	1865
JC 403	Straus, Joseph	Kobler, John	1865
JC 31	Stubled, James et al	People of the State	1863
JC 53	Swearinger, Samuel	LeRoy, A.R.	1865
JC 77	Swearinger, Samuel	Breed, L.N.	1864
JC 222	Swearinger, Samuel	Adams, Abijah	1864
JC 453	Swearinger, Samuel	Byers, James D.	1865
JC 78	Swearinger, Samuel et al	Stark, Lewis	1864
JC 143	Swearinger, Samuel et al	Davis, S.	1863
JC 392	Tefft, H.	Roop, I.N.	1867
JC 401	Tefft, Hiram	Lander, Boson	1864
JC 213	Thayer, George A.	Clark, C.B.	1864
JC 134	Thompson, H.F.	Hosselkus, E.D.	1863
JC 135	Thompson, H.F.	Dake, C.W.	1863
JC 150	Thompson, H.F.	Giddings, C.	1863
JC 151	Thompson, H.F.	Long & Leroy	1863
JC 387	Thompson, H.F.	Davis, S.	1863
JC 63	Thompson, H.F. et al	Hosselkus & Harvey	1865
JC 84	Thompson, Manley	Barnes, Truman	1864
JC 355	Thompson, Richard	People of the State	1867
JC 255	Thompson, U.T.	Brannon, E.	1862
JC 345	Toladay, John	People of the State	1865
JC 1	Townsend, E.	Smith, A.A.	1866
JC 332	True, T. et al	People of the State	1866
JD 14	Tucker, John	Storff, Antone	1861
JC 478	Tunnel, S.P.	Adams, Abijah	1867
JC 90	Tusler, E. & Bro.	People of the State	1865
JC 14	Tyrell, Henry	Harris, Jackson	1866

Case #	Defendant	Plaintiff	Year
JC 242	Tyler, Jerry	Todd, Edward	1866
JD 4	Tyler, Jerry	People of the State	1861
JC 96	Tyron & Brother	People of the State	1865
JC 107	Vaden, E.	Bates, H.P.	1867
JC 114	Vance, E.W.	Clemmons & Myers	1867
JC 110	Vance, E.W. et al	Johnson, O.N.	1867
JC 111	Vance, E.W. et al	People of the State	1867
JC 39	Van Kirk, William	People of the State	1865
JC 125	Varney, E.L.	Slater, John A.	1862
JC 423	Vaughn, A.M.	People of the State	1865
JC 32	Vincent, Dow	Kyle, C.A.	1865
JC 230	Vincent, Dow	Hamilton & Cornell	1864
JC 110	Vincent, G.H.B. et al	Johnson, O.N.	1867
JC 91	Walbridge, H.W.	People of the State	1865
JC 234	Walbridge, H.W. et al	Sneath & Bowman	1868
JC 142	Wales, Philip	Stinson, S.	1863
JC 45	Walker, G.W.	Clemmons, W.W.	1865
JC 211	Walker, William	People of the State	1864
JC 43	Walker, William C.	People of the State	1865
JC 2	Ward, John S.	Susanville Fire Co.	1866
JC 384	Washburn, Griffin & Co.	People of the State	1867
JC 37	Waterland, W.	Giddings, C.	1865
JC 426	Weatherlow, William	People of the State	1865
JD 8	Weatherlow, William	Nichols, E.R.	1861
JC 124	Webb, John	People of the State	1862
JC 370	Webb, John	Ward, John S.	1862
JC 178	Wedekind, George L.	Nelson, A.H.	1864
JC 183	Wedekind, George L.	Peyser, S.	1864
JC 202	Wedekind, George L.	Hardin, A.W.	1864
JC 230	Wedekind, John	Williams, John A.	1864
JC 118	Wentworth, Wm.	Sloss, F.A.	1867
JC 232	Wentworth, William	People of the State	1864
JC 394	Wentworth, William	Roop, I.N.	1863
JD 11	White, W.	Bare, Thomas	1861
JC 447	Whitney, C.S.	People of the State	1863
JC 204	Westfall, J.W.	Ford, William	1864

Case #	Defendant	Plaintiff	Year
JC 480	Wiggin, J.M.	Lattin, Samuel	1866
JC 64	Wilcox, H.K.	People of the State	1864
JC 46	Wilmans, D.I.	Southworth, L.	1865
JC 193	Wilmans, D.I.	Hosselkus & Harvey	1864
JC 195	Wilmans, D.I.	Purdom, T.C.	1864
JC 419	Wilmans, D.I.	People of the State	1865
JC 42	Wilmans, D.I. et al	Hines, Fred	1865
JC 399	Williams & Blake	Tipton & Burt	1867
JC 139	Williams, Frank et al	Pond, E.B.	1863
JC 411	Williams, Jno.	People of the State	1864
JC 461	Williams, Jno.	People of the State	1865
JC 36	Wills, John	People of the State	1865
JC 437	Wilson, T.C.	Wentworth, William	1864
JC 167	Winchell, H. et al	Perry, Geo. W.	1863
JD 26	Winchell, H. et al	Lake, M.C.	1863
JC 427	Winn, M.	People of the State	1865
JC 223	Wright, A.D.	Sanders, W.	1864
JC 417	Wright, A.S.	People of the State	1865
JC 246	Wright, John	People of the State	1867
JC 33	Wright, P.	People of the State	1863
JD 31	Wright, Patrick et al	People of the State	1863
JC 40	Wooly, William	People of the State	1865

ACKNOWLEDGEMENTS

First of all an explanation of the "Menopause Manor" referred to in the "Dedication." Menopause Manor and Bruce were a delightful bunch of people that worked in the Lassen County Clerk's office from the time I was associated with them in 1975, until their various departures by 1986, though Bruce still remains there. Menopause Manor was their own satirical nickname. Under their guidance I was provided with a wonderful education in county government and the court system. Thank you Sue Farstad, Jacquelyn Fuller, Betty Hibbs, June Nelson and my old side kick, Bruce Dyer.

In the photograph department I would like to extend my thanks to the following people for use of the illustrations: Ivajean Brietwieser, Gil Morrill, Helene Andrews, Janet Corey of the Lassen County Historical Society and the Nevada Historical Society.

In the final production stages I am indebted to Chris Geffre who relieved me of the burden of typesetting and page counts. Finally, a very special thanks to Cindy LoBuglio, my ever faithful editor.

ABOUT THE AUTHOR

Tim I. Purdy is a native of Susanville and not only is he the sixth generation of his family to live in California, but in Lassen County as well!

Early in life he became fascinated with the history of Northeastern California from listening to the many stories told to him by the old timers. This, of course, with his inquisitive nature, caused him to research some of these tall tales related to him--only to his amazement to find out that many of the stories were true. Thus, came the discovery that there was a wealth of material of the region's rich heritage that not only needed to be researched and saved, but also to be set down in writing and preserved for future generations.

Today, the author is actively involved with a wide variety of organizations dedicated to historical preservation. He conducts historical research for both individuals and institutions and with his company, Lahontan Images, he publishes and distributes books pertaining to Northeastern California.

BIBLIOGRAPHY

Aiken, Charles Curry, *The Sagebrush War: The California-Nevada Boundary Dispute on the 120th. Meridian* (thesis) University of Oklahoma, Norman, Oklahoma, 1971.

Davis, W.N. Jr., *California Indians V: The Sagebrush Corner. The Opening of California's Northeast*, New York: Garland Publishing, 1974.

Fairfield, Asa M., *Fairfield's Pioneer History of Lassen County, California*, San Francisco: H.S. Crocker Co., 1916,

Farris & Smith, *The History of Lassen, Plumas and Sierra Counties, California, 1882*, Berkeley: Howell-North, 1971.

INDEX

Thompson, Sarah 40-41
Titherington, David 24
Toll Roads 15-16, 58-59
Tucker, Dutch Johnny 23-24
Tule Confederacy 46-47
Tyler, Elizabeth 30, 40
Tyler, Jerry 30, 40, 58

-U-
Utah Territory 3, 15, 51

-V-
VanKirk, William 44
Vary, Ladue 17
Vincent, Dow 22-23
Virginia City, Nevada 3, 15-16

-W-
Wales, Philip 8-9
Walker, William 26
Ward, John S. 4, 21, 22-23, 26, 65, 68-69
Washoe County, Nevada 5
Water Rights 23-24
Weatherlow, William 16-17, 23, 52, 54-55
Webb, John 26-27
Wedekind, George 20-21
Wentworth, William 26
White, M.G. 9
White, W. 17-18
Whitney, C.S. 26
Williams, Jesse 30
Williams, John 30
Winnemucca, Nevada 10

-Y-
Young, William J. 18, 21, 25, 26, 27, 28, 29, 47, 69, 70